GW00646667

Live Oaks & Gentle Folks

Published in cooperation with the Montrose Garden Club
Copyright American Image Publishing 2003

Corporate Leaders

The Montrose Garden Club gratefully acknowledges these corporate leaders, who have made the publishing of Live Oaks and Gentle Folks a reality.

About the Cover Artist

Blanche Sumrall paints traditional subject matter with a devotion to intrinsic details and jewel-tone colors—details and vivacious colors reminiscent of the Old Masters in their ability to stir warmth and emotion.

Sumrall's unique realistic style combines the vitality of Old Masters with the techniques of today's finest water colorists. Exhibiting both internationally and nationally, Blanche has many limited-edition prints and her original and commissioned pieces are in demand by both private and corporate collectors. Her art gallery, B Sumrall Art Gallery, is located in Fairhope.

Contents

Published by American Image Publishing copyright 2003 in cooperation with the Montrose Garden Club
Executive Editors: James E. Turner, Joe O'Donnell • American Image Publishing, Birmingham, Alabama • www.amimage.net
Printed in the USA by American Printing Company, Birmingham, Alabama
ISBN 9741374-2-1

Live Oaks Gentle Folks

Live oak grove photo by Charlie Siefried (courtesy First National Bank of Baldwin County)

Foreword

Southern ladies and gentlemen find in Baldwin County, Alabama a comfortable place… a gentle place… and a place filled with delicious stories, interesting characters, and above all… recipes from many different cultural traditions.

The magnificent Baldwin County Live Oak trees gracefully spread large meandering branches over narrow neighborhood roads. Those trees are the reason for this book. A small group of ladies in Montrose, Alabama, have protected the trees for more than fifty years. Now they are working to encourage the care and maintenance of these priceless treasures throughout Baldwin County.

This is a book to be savored. Spend some quiet times reflecting on the tradition rich county that is much older than the state of Alabama. Celebrate festive occasions with the people of the South. The reader will tour historic landmarks, explore hidden architectural treasures, see Baldwin County through the eyes of the artist, and savor warm afternoon teas at the Grand Hotel Marriott. In the pages of this book, you'll also learn about fascinating local businesses that give Baldwin County its unique flavor and flair.

Live Oaks and Gentle Folks is not just a book… it is a way of life… so enjoy this book and your time in Baldwin County at a leisurely pace. And tempt yourself with some of the wonderful recipes collected here.

Introduction

Everyone thinks the place they live is special, and everyone is right. There are things about each town, city, neighborhood, crossroads, and farm that make each unique, that makes the wind in the trees, the traffic on the street below, the quiet call of a morning bird sing out with the comforting phrase: this is home.

Well, this is our home, Baldwin County. Journey with us now as we traverse this place in our heart—this corner of Alabama. So diverse. So exciting. And so quietly dignified. Baldwin County is all of these things and so very much more.

According to the 2000 census, there are 140,415 souls living here. Bordered by the Gulf of Mexico, Mobile Bay and the forests and fields of Alabama and northwest Florida, Baldwin County—established in 1809—is older than the state itself, founded while Alabama was still officially a part of the Mississippi territory.

Ironically, the county—one of the largest in land mass east of the Mississippi River—was named for a Connecticut Revolutionary War veteran, lawyer, politician and educator named Abraham Baldwin. Baldwin had moved to Georgia to practice law and later founded and served as the first president of the University of Georgia. The county was named in his honor.

That's history. This is today.

Pitch a tent on the banks of a clear-running stream deep within a pristine forest. Wiggle your toes in the world's softest and whitest sand while Gulf waters eddy around your ankles. Hunt white-tailed deer or quail in the uplands. Sample fine wines at Alabama's largest winery, Perdido Vineyards. Taste homemade cheese varieties from Cajun to chocolate at Alabama's only licensed cheese farm, Sweet Home Farms in Elberta. Munch delectable candies and preserves from old family recipes at Punta Clara Kitchen and family museum. Step back in time to the largest Indian massacre at Fort Mims, where the death toll exceeded that of General Custer's forces at Little Big Horn.

Charter a boat, watch professional theater, shop at one of the largest factory outlets in the South, play golf or tennis, ride a horse along the beach, build a sandcastle, or canoe a winding stream. In fact, do just about anything that rates the definition "fun" without requiring snow and ice. The unequaled recreational opportunities available in this vast, culturally diverse county are a main reason more people are coming home to Baldwin County.

Located in Lillian is the Perdido Bay Campground Resort, a KOA affiliate that provides just about everything you would want to do at a campground.

There are air conditioned cabins, a tent area, recreation and game room, plenty of outdoor sports facilities including shuffleboard, volleyball, basketball, a pool, and a boating and fishing pier.

The campground is open year-round and offers reasonable rates. The Perdido Bay Campground Resort's motto is "Camp where the Spaniards did under 200-year old oaks on historic Perdido Bay."

At the smack of a mallet and ball, polo ponies thunder across a manicured green under a Kodachrome sky. Champagne glasses clink and cheers break forth along the sidelines. Moments later golden October light bathes the field as Great Britain's Polo Team—led by Maj. Ronald

Copy adapted from www.siteone.com. Used by permission.

Path through live oaks photo by Charlie Siefried (courtesy First National Bank of Baldwin County)

*Live Oaks
Gentle Folks*

Magnolia Bluff circa 1834 *watercolor by Ann Durrett (from the collection of Lois and Jack Boykin)*

loons, and a sailing regatta provide colorful backdrops for the throngs who stroll the beaches lined with concessionaires of succulent seafood. This is Baldwin County on the same Sunday afternoon.

A highway hamburger stand in Robertsdale looks like any other fast-food restaurant until you spot the rack of personal coffee mugs behind the counter, indicating this is more to the residents than a grab and gulp stop. At one table, three prosperous-looking farmers reminisce about their childhoods a half-century ago. Conversation lags at the other tables as residents and strangers eavesdrop on vignettes of long-ago marble games when lunches were toted to school in lard cans. The audience brings out the best in the storytellers who scoot their chairs around for better eye contact. Before long the scene resembles an old country store without the pot-bellied stove or pickle barrels. Fluorescent lights, air conditioning and modern decor do not inhibit the old-time camaraderie developing among the patrons. It's still Baldwin County on the same Sunday afternoon.

The diversity of lifestyles in Baldwin County defies all

Ferguson, father of the Duchess of York—concedes defeat to the Point Clear Polo Team. This is Baldwin County on a Sunday afternoon.

Just 50 miles south, a four-day blitz of art, culture and seafood sampling winds down at the Annual Shrimp Festival in Gulf Shores. Thousands of people have come from neighboring states to enjoy jazz, gospel, Cajun, and steel drum music. Native American dancers, cloggers and outstanding modern dance troupes have shared the stage with dozens of other performers. Visual art of every medium, hot air bal-

stereotypes. There is, quite simply, no other place like it. At 110 miles long and an average 20 miles wide, Baldwin County is one of the largest U. S. counties east of the Mississippi River. Within its boundaries the landscape changes from a glittering Gulf Coast of sparkling water and snow white beaches into a rolling farmland and deep forest threaded by fresh water creeks too numerous to have names. Perhaps the landscapes set the tone for living, because every lifestyle is available to county residents except the harried rat race of the big city. Creativity flourishes amid countless performing and visual art groups. Vast spaces of undeveloped land are still available for those who want to raise livestock or agricultural crops. The laid-back atmosphere of the Gulf Coast invites new residents and new businesses to serve the increasing demand of tourists. Friendly small towns and unincorporated communities are scattered throughout the county, ready to welcome newcomers into their schools, civic clubs and churches.

First or second careers are waiting for people who have always wanted to develop a tennis resort, manage a fish camp, own a pecan grove, work on a charter boat, start a desk-top publishing company, set up a manufacturing or distribution company, market a new invention, plan an upscale retirement community, or relocate a construction company to a place where mild winters allow year-round building. Opportunities in Baldwin County are limited only by your imagination.

France, Italy, Greece, Germany, Yugoslavia, Russia,

Sweden, Czechoslovakia and a dozen other countries have contributed to the county's ancestry, making it a thoroughly American melting pot of fine people. Working together in agriculture, tourism, manufacturing and fishing to make their county prosper, they possess an attitude of perseverance and goodwill that is unique. Museums, parks, historical landmarks and annual festivals pay tribute to their heritage.

Affordable real estate and some of the lowest property taxes in the nation help young families and retirees choose Baldwin County for their new homes. From undeveloped wilderness to totally maintained resort developments, there is property available in Baldwin County for every taste and pocketbook

Listen... to the satisfying "plop" of a sinker dropping into the dawn-colored water of a backwoods fishing hole. Or the splash of hooves galloping through the surf. Or the creak of the mast as a fresh breeze fills the sails on your catamaran. Feel... the pull of that big snapper, the last catch of the day before the chartered boat heads toward shore for the night... or the cool shade within a historic fort, just as welcome today as it was for Civil War soldiers stationed there. Smell... the sharp, green cypress fragrance of ancient forests; a fisherman's tarred nets drying in the hot sun; a faint scent of lavender in Victorian linens at an antique shop. See... a glamorous midway under the stars; or alligators, sea turtles and exotic birds in protected natural habitats. Recreation in Baldwin County awakens all the senses with a variety of choices unmatched anywhere.

A Tour of Baldwin County

Travel with us now as we experience the sites, history, cuisine, and culture in the land of live oaks and gentle folks. We'll begin in the northern reaches of Baldwin County...

Path through live oaks photo by Charlie Siefried (courtesy First National Bank of Baldwin County)

Old Montgomery Hill Baptist Church *painting by Cleve Woodard (courtesy of Charlie and Pat Earle)*

Live Oaks
Gentle Folks

Tensaw

Over 10,000 years ago, the prehistoric aborigines were the earliest known people to inhabit what is now known as Baldwin County. Next came the Shellmound people and then the Early Woodlanders, around the birth of Christ.

When the First Europeans came to the American shores, the Alabama Indians were on hand to greet them. Some of the Indian tribes were the Cherokee, Choctaw, Chickasaw, Creeks and the Tensas. The Tensas Indians moved in from Louisiana and settled on the banks of the Tensaw River, but the Creeks soon dominated the area.

The first American settlement in Baldwin was made on the banks of Lake Tensaw and the Alabama River. Lake Tensaw was originally called the arm of the sea, as it is a branch of the Tensaw River after it meets the Delta. Here on the banks of the Tensaw River, Major Robert Farmar developed a plantation in 1772. Farmar was one of the most prominent and controversial Alabamians of the British period, being commander of the regiments at Mobile from 1763-1765. He resigned his commission in 1768 and was elected to every Commons House of Assembly for the District of West Florida from 1769 until his death in 1778. Artist-Naturalist, William Bartram, visited Farmar in 1775 and recorded the plant life of the area. As the appointed botanist of Britain's King George III, Bartram traveled 2,400 miles in three journeys into the southern colonies in 1775-1776, collecting rare plants and specimens and making detailed drawings of plants and animals. This journey was called Bartram's Trail.

The earliest known school in the state of Alabama was located in Tensaw on Boatyard Lake and was known as the Boatyard School. John Pierce founded it in 1799 to teach the children of the wealthy planters and lumbermen.

Many of the early families are still in the county today: Byrne, Easley, Steadham, Hall, Mims, Pierce, Sibley and Holmes. Later the Scots arrived and a Lachlan McGillivray married Sehoy Marchard, whose mother was a member of the Wind Clan, one of the most powerful Creek Indian families. This helped Lachlan to become an influential leader of the Creeks. A son, Alexander, was born of this union. He was the uncle of Red Eagle, Indian Chief William Weatherford. Red Eagle, one of the most famous Indian warriors, died in 1824 at the age of 60 and is buried in North Baldwin County.

Andrew Jackson built a home, Montpelier, in north Baldwin which he lived in for two years, while he searched for Red Eagle.

Tensaw today is a remote area, located on Alabama Highway 59, north of Bay Minette. Local residents see the remoteness as an advantage and enjoy being away from a bustling town. The 2000 Census recorded 225 residents in Tensaw.

Fort Mims

On August 30, 1813 the Creek Indians staged an attack in which more than 500 men, women and children were killed. Today this scenic, five-acre park on County Road 80 off of Highway 59 in Tensaw is preserved as an historic site. Each August, an event commemorating the battle is held by the Ft. Mims Restoration Association. Admission to the park is free and self-guided tours lead visitors to points of historic interest.

Stockton

Stockton was founded in 1834 and incorporated in 1839. The town of Stockton grew up around the stagecoach. William Kitchen and Ward Taylor became partners in the Southwest Alabama Stagecoach Line. The stagecoach routes ran throughout Alabama. A four-horse stagecoach made daily trips between Montgomery and Blakely, a 192-mile trip that took 43 hours to complete. The line placed more than 200 horses in five-acre pastures at intervals of approximately 16 miles—allowing for the exchange of fresh horses.

Stagecoach stops in Baldwin County included Little River, Montgomery Hill (now Tensaw), the Patrick Byrnes Tavern near Blakely and in Stockton. The Hammond family in Stockton operated a stagecoach depot, and the attic of the building became sleeping quarters for weary travelers.

In 1854, Kitchen and his wife, Narcissia, built a house in Stockton that included an immense carriage house and a tiny post office.

Stagecoach Café

A restaurant where life moves at a slower pace, the Stagecoach Café in Stockton offers visitors a daily buffet of home-style meats and vegetables, as well as homey rocking chairs on the front porch. Here you'll find the freshest seafood as well as delectable steaks.

Recipe

Stagecoach Café Peach Cobbler

4 cups	sugar
4 cups	self-rising flour
1 tsp.	baking powder
	milk
1 lb.	margarine
1 gal.	peaches

Mix flour, sugar and baking powder, then mix in milk (enough for batter to look like a cake mix). Melt margarine, adding first to batter, peaches last.
Bake at 325 to 350 degrees for 1 hour to 1 hour and 15 minutes. Feeds 30 people.

Submitted by Care House, Inc. courtesy of Stagecoach Café

Live Oaks Gentle Folks

Best Spot *watercolor by Wayne Spradley (courtesy of the artist)*

Baldwin County Commission

Baldwin County, Alabama, located on the shores of the Gulf of Mexico and Mobile Bay, is bordered on the West by Mobile County, Alabama, on the Northwest by Washington County, Alabama, and Clarke County, Alabama, on the North by Monroe County, Alabama, on the Northeast by Escambia County, Alabama, and on the East by Escambia County, Florida.

While the county has twelve incorporated municipalities, ranging in size and density, a majority of Baldwin County's 140,415 residents reside in rural, unincorporated areas.

The county government is headquartered at the county seat in the City of Bay Minette and is governed by a seven member county commission with all seven members elected by single-member county commission districts.

The current County Commissioners are Chairman Frank Burt, Jr. [(R) - District 2: Northeast & Northcentral Baldwin County]; Vice Chairman George A. Price [(R) - District 3: Westcentral, Central & Eastcentral Baldwin County]; Commissioner Jonathan H. Armstrong [(R) - District 1: Northwest, West & Westcentral Baldwin County]; Commissioner Mary Frances Stewart [(R) - District 4: Southcentral Baldwin County]; Commissioner Charles A. Browdy [(R) - District 5: South Baldwin County]; Commissioner David E. Bishop [(R) - District 6: Southwest Baldwin County & Southern Eastern Shore]; Commissioner Allen D. Perdue [(R) - District 7: West Baldwin County & Northern Eastern Shore].

The county's twelve municipalities are operated under the mayor/council form of government with most municipalities electing council members pursuant to at-large elections, few municipalities electing council members by single-member districts, all municipalities electing Mayors from at-large elections and some municipalities employing city administrators. The county's public school system includes all public schools in the unincorporated & incorporated areas and is governed by a seven member board of education elected from single-member districts.

Baldwin County remains a popular destination for visitors year round because of first class golf courses, beautiful beaches, and unlimited recreational opportunities.

The county is blessed with a health economy and first class public school system which contributes to our explosive population growth since the 1990's. Today, out of Alabama's sixty-seven counties, Baldwin County remains one of the top three fastest growing.

Recipes

Nancy Pilot's Grits

8 slices bacon
1   onion
1   green pepper
1/4 tsp.   sugar
1   16 oz. can of tomatoes (undrained)
6 cups   water
1 tsp.   salt
1 1/2 cps. uncooked grits
grated cheese to taste

Saute onions and pepper, stir in tomatoes and sugar. Bring to boil and simmer. Cook grits in water and salt. Stir in tomato mixture. pour in casserole and sprinkle with bacon and cheese. Bake at 350 degrees, 20 to 30 minutes.
Submitted by Nancy Pilot

Small Pound Cake

1 cup   butter
1 2/3 cps sugar
6   eggs
2 cups   flour
1 tsp.   flavoring lemon or vanilla or both

Cream butter. Add sugar and cream until grains have disappeared. Add 1 egg at a time and beat well each time. Add flour slowly as you beat and keep the sides scraped. Add flavoring. Bake in tube pan at 325 degrees for 1 hour or until cake springs back to touch.

Baked Custard

4 cups   milk scalded
1/2 cup   sugar
4 to 6   eggs
1/4 tsp.   salt
1 tsp.   vanilla

Beat eggs slightly. Add sugar and salt. Add the scalded milk slowly to egg mixture. Add vanilla. Strain into buttered molds and set in a pan of hot water. Bake in 325 degree oven until firm. If a silver knife comes out clean, the custard is done. Submitted by Mrs. Cecil Agnew Thompson

Fried Yellow Catfish Filets

Dip filets in lite beer or Coca-Cola. Drain. Sprinkle well with Cavender's Greek Seasoning. When you think there is enough seasoning, add more. Marinate one hour. Dredge filets in mixture of one-half yellow corn meal and one-half plain flour. Deep fry in peanut oil heated to 400 degrees. About one minute before removal, put three slices of onion on top of fish. When temperature of oil drops to 300 degrees remove fish and serve. Submitted by Clyde "Buddy" Steele

Choice Deer Roast (may substitute beef)

Season heavily with salt, pepper and garlic salt. Put roast in Dutch oven. Add 1 to 1 1/2 Cokes depending on roast size. Add 1 cup Del Monte Cajun style stewed tomatoes. Quarter 3 potatoes and 3 onions and add to roast. Cover and cook at 300 degrees for 3 hours. Add enough rice to soak up gravy. Cook 20 minutes more with lid on. Submitted by Clyde "Buddy" Steele

North Baldwin Barn and Wagon *painting by Don Reber (courtesy of Jim and Annette Lay)*

Live Oaks
Gentle Folks

December Solitude *painting by Donny Finley (courtesy of Jim and Annette Lay)*

Baked Salmon with Feta

2	green onions chopped
3 tsp.	butter
2	tomatoes, chopped
1 tsp.	rosemary
1/2 tsp.	salt
	red pepper flakes to taste
4-5 ozs.	salmon filets
4 tbsp.	feta or goat cheese crumbles

Saute onions in butter until tender. Add tomato, rosemary, salt and red pepper. Cook until tender. Place salmon in pam sprayed baking dish and cover with tomato mixture, top with cheese and bake until fish flakes at 350 degrees for about 20 minutes. Submitted by Dorothy Bodiford

Doves & Gravy

3 tbsp.	oil
1 cup	flour
	salt, pepper
	chopped onion to cover
	chicken broth to cover

Season dove and flour. Brown floured dove in hot oil. Do not cook. Remove and drain. Sauté onion in drippings. Place broth in skillet over onions to make gravy. Place dove in casserole dish and cover with gravy and onions. Cook in 325-degree oven for 1 1/2 hours or until tender and gravy thickens. Serve over hot grits with greens and cornbread. Submitted by Steve McMillan

CARE House

The turn-of-the-century Woodson family home at 108 Blackburn Avenue in Bay Minette was donated to CARE House in 1986. This historic facility opened its doors as the Baldwin County Child Advocacy Center and began serving abused children in the spring of 1989.

Each year over 500 child victims and their families are provided services through the center while ongoing prevention, awareness and education information is available to all—so that together we can stop future victimization of our children. The generosity of the Woodson family and the sensitivity and deep caring of all of our Baldwin County citizens lives on each day in the heritage of CARE House.

Bradley Byrne

The Byrne Family's roots in Baldwin County reach back to the 1780's when patriarch Gerald Byrne settled in the area around Byrne's Lake now present day Bromley. Gerald's son Patrick was Baldwin County's first Probate Judge, and Gerald II was an early Postmaster. Other descendents have served as circuit judges and most recently Gerald's Great-Great-Great-Grandson Bradley was elected State Senator. The Byrnes are a good example of Baldwin County's early families whose traditions of service have endured over two centuries.

Blakeley

The streets of Blakeley were paved in brick and carried the traffic of residents, businessmen, travelers, and tourists to their appointments, homes, places of business and the Alabama Hotel, the largest hotel in the vast Mississippi Territory. Founded by Josiah Blakeley in 1814, the community was settled by Americans from New England. The first county seat was at McIntosh Bluff on the Tombigbee, but was moved to Blakeley in 1820.

The young town was fast becoming an industrial center, with its steam boat company and most important, its port facilities which sent cotton up the Tensaw River and to points all over the United States.

The protected harbor was gradually pulling away from Mobile's port trade. Fresh water springs meant prosperity for settlers. Doctors, lawyers and other professionals hung out their shingles in this promising town.

The state's first newspapers were started here, the Blakeley Sun and Alabama Advertiser.

From 1820 to 1830, the town slowly died. An epidemic of malaria and yellow fever took thousands of lives. Out of greed, the price of land went up and the would-be chance to help save the town pushed investors away. The dredging of Choctaw Pass in the Mobile Port made it easier for ships to enter the port of Mobile rather than Blakeley's.

{The Battle of Blakeley Festival is held in Blakeley State Park the first weekend in April. Since 1979, the Blakeley Cajun Bluegrass Festival has been held the first Saturday in October at the state park.}

In spite of the failure of the town, the county seat remained in Blakeley until 1868.

During the Civil War, a makeshift fort, housing about 3,500 Confederate soldiers, was built in Blakeley. The last battle of the Civil War was fought here.

Bay Minette

An associate of the French founders of Mobile, Minet mapped what was to become Baldwin County in the 1700s. He originally called Bay Minette, Minette Bay. The first settlers to live in the present-day Bay Minette came during the Civil War. By 1881, the town was thriving.

A lumberman from New England by the name of J.D. Hand raised $35,000 to build the first courthouse, the opening salvo in a bid to move the county seat to Bay Minette. Hand organized the midnight escapade in which townspeople invaded Daphne in an attempt to hijack the seat of county government. The citizens took the county records and even the furniture.

Bay Minette has been the county seat since 1901. In 1907 the town was incorporated. The city has grown around the picturesque Courthouse Square, where all roads leading into Bay Minette meet and circle at the courthouse.

Standard Furniture is one of the oldest businesses in the city. It was opened in 1946 by the Hodgson Family and manufactured bedroom furniture. Now it carries a diverse line of furniture, including imported pieces. Bay Minette is also home to James H. Faulkner State Community College.

Spanish Fort

In history books, the Civil War ended weeks before the Battles of Spanish Fort and Blakeley. Because of slow communication, word had not reached South Alabama on April 9, 1865, when the surrender took place.

But this was not the first battle that took place at Spanish Fort, for the area saw action in the Revolutionary War and the War of 1812. Spanish Fort was a defense site for Spanish soldiers defending Mobile from British troops trying to recapture the city of Mobile.

High on a hill overlooking Mobile Bay, rests Spanish Fort. Baldwin County's newest city, incorporated in 1993, is fast growing in population and land mass. New shopping centers as well as many new homes are springing up.

You can still find carefully preserved breastworks from the Civil War as well as remains of Red Mounds used to collect Union bullets and for protection. Almost all bullets are of Union origin, because the South had no resources of its own and used ammunition stolen from the enemy. Relic hunters have over the years collected bullets, cannon ball fragments, buttons, and belt buckles just to name a few.

Malbis Church

Constructed at a cost of more than $1 million back in the 1960s, this Greek Orthodox Church was built on the plantation of Greek immigrant Jason Malbis. With many of the architectural elements of this grand house of worship shipped from Greece, the church is an historical treasure.

Daphne

Artifacts and burial sites of prehistoric mounds indicate settlement in this area dates back as early as 1500. One of the first settlers was Louis D'Olive, a Frenchman who had a nearby plantation. Andrew Jackson marched through Daphne while hunting down the famous Indian chief Red Eagle. History records that he addressed his troops under the boughs of a giant oak tree just south of Daphne. Today that area is known as Jackson Oaks.

Originally the town was built on the waterfront with a bustling port facility. When the causeway was opened in 1927, the town began to move up the "hill." A favorite saying from these times was "They're moving everything up the hill... the bay will be next."

The bay boats were a vital part of Daphne, bringing tourists to the Howard Hotel, now Bayside Academy, a private school.

In 1886 the county courthouse was constructed.

Malbis Greek Orthodox Church

Before the courthouse's construction, court sessions were held on the ground of the Howard Hotel under a large oak. After the controversy regarding the move of the county records to Bay Minette, angry men, who were going to the North Baldwin town to retrieve the records, decided to have a drink and cool off. After a few drinks, the anger passed and the men decided they no longer wanted to have the county seat in Daphne.

The first Italian who came to the Belforest-Daphne area was Alesandro Mastro Valerio. Here land could be bought for $1.50 to $5 an acre. Other families soon followed: the Sibleys, Allegri, Campbell, Edmondson, Manci, Trione, and Corte.

When the Italians came, there was no Catholic church in which to worship. Services were held in the Giacomovich home and continued there, even after the home was sold to Giovanni Predazzer. In 1890, the Church of the Assumption

Judge Roy Bean's, *watercolor by Christine Linson (courtesy of the artist)*

was built, later replaced by Christ the King in 1937. In 1949 an elementary school was built, fulfilling a dream of Father Angelo Chiariglione, who served as parish priest from 1890 to 1908. A new church was built in 1993. Names of the original Italian colonists and many of their descendents are etched on paving tiles in front of the new church.

D'Olive Nature Trail

Take a walk down the D'Olive Plantation Nature Trail to see history preserved. Along the way you'll see one of the largest oaks in Alabama, two state champion trees, historic Yancey Branch and the D'Olive cemetery which dates to the late 18th century.

*Live Oaks
Gentle Folks*

Recipes

Greek Salad
(serves 12)

1/2 cup   extra virgin olive oil
3 tbsp.   red wine vinegar
3 tbsp.   lemon juice (if desired)
2 tbsp.   chopped oregano
           salt and freshly ground pepper to taste
4   romaine lettuce, torn or iceberg lettuce
6-7   cucumbers (peeled and sliced 1/2 inch thick)
6-7   medium tomatoes (cut into small wedges)
1/2 lb.   feta cheese, crumbled (about 1 1/2 cups, may add more if desired)
1 cup   black kalamata olives

Mix together the olive oil, vinegar, lemon juice (if desired) and sprinkle with oregano. Add salt and pepper. You may use a Greek salad dressing from the grocery store instead of the above dressing. Mix in a bowl the lettuce, cucumbers, tomatoes, cheese and olives. Toss salad with the dressing and it's ready to serve.

Xoriatiki
(traditional Greek village salad)
serves 7

5   ripe tomatoes
2   cucumbers
1   onion
1   green bell pepper
1 cup   kalamata olives
           oregano
           salt
1/3 lb.   crumbled feta cheese
1/2 cup   olive oil

Cut vegetables into slices and mix in a bowl. Top with the olives and oregano and cover with crumbled feta cheese. Pour the olive oil evenly over the top. Serve with hot bread.

Tzatziki
Cucumber spread

4   cucumbers
3 clvs.   garlic, peeled and minced
3 tbsp.   olive oil
           salt and pepper to taste
1 cup   yogurt and 1 cup sour cream mixed together
           vinegar to taste if desired

Peel and remove seeds from cucumbers. Put cucumbers through fine grater (do not use a blender). Drain grated cucumber in a colander until juices stop running. (If needed use a paper towel to pat excess water from the grated cucumber). In a bowl, mash the garlic with the olive oil, salt and pepper. Stir in the cucumbers and yogurt/sour cream. Chill covered for 2 to 3 hours. Serve as a dip with crackers, raw vegetables, fresh bread or pita.
Submitted by Eleni Tsaltsa

The Wharf *watercolor by Jo Patton (courtesy of Sally Lieberman)*

Live Oaks
Gentle Folks

Recipes

Polenta

Polenta with Bird Gravy
(also made with beef, pork, rabbit or chicken) submitted by
Mrs. V.J. (Vic Rolando) Allegri, Sr.)

12-15	doves
8 tbsp.	olive oil
1 med.	onion, chopped
1 clove	garlic, chopped
1/4 tsp.	salt
1/8 tsp.	pepper
1 med.	can tomatoes
2 small	cans tomato paste
1 can	water

Place olive oil, onion, garlic in large skillet, brown gently.
Add salt, pepper, tomatoes, puree water, birds and simmer 1
1/2 hours or until you can remove the bones of the birds.
When gravy is ready, take:

1 lb.	cornmeal
1 1/4 qts.	boiling water
3 tsp.	salt
3 tbsp.	grated romano cheese

Mix cornmeal with cold water and pour slowly into boiling
salted water, stirring constantly with wooden spoon.
Continue cooking and stirring 30 minutes or until cornmeal
leaves sides of pan easily. Pour cornmeal onto large platter,

pour gravy over it, and sprinkle with cheese. Serves 4 to 6.

Pasta Con Melanzana
(pasta with eggplant)

Prepare eggplant by cutting into cubes about 3/4 inch. Salt
and drain for 1 to 2 hours. Sauté in olive oil or any vegetable
oil until lightly browned. Put into basic tomato sauce which
has been simmering about 1/2 hour. (Sauce should be thick
because eggplant will add liquid to the sauce) Cook eggplant
and sauce about 45 minutes on low heat. Serve generously on
the cooked pasta. (This makes an excellent dish for meatless
Fridays)

Basic sauce for pasta: Sauté about 1/4 onion and 2 cloves of
garlic which have been chopped up. Add a quart of cooked,
strained tomatoes and a small can of tomato paste. Season
with salt and 1 or 2 teaspoons of sugar (enough sugar to
remove high acidity). Cook slowly about an hour until thick
and tasty. Toward end add 1 or 2 leaves of Sweet Basil. Pasta
should be cooked in a separate pot and well-drained before
covering with thick sauce.

Meat sauce: (beef roast or pork shoulder or meatballs) Brown
roast lightly. Put into basic sauce for cooking. (30 to 45 minutes in a pressure cooker depending on size) Meatballs
should be sautéed before putting in sauce. Simmer 30 to 45
minutes. Our family likes a small piece of pork shoulder
cooked in the sauce and then meatballs added.
Submitted by Mrs. Agostino (Mary Lazzari) Guarisco

Interior of Manci's store (courtesy of Alex Manci)

Manci's Antique Club

The building that now houses Manci's was a complex of businesses first built in the early 1900s by Frank Manci and Angelo Trione. The north side of the complex was originally a produce warehouse and later a gas station. The family owned two Model T Fords that were used as taxis, picking up passengers off the bay boats coming to the Eastern Shore from Mobile. Later Frank's son, Arthur Manci, opened a bar, filling it with interesting photographs, bottles and artifacts—that was the beginning of Manci's Antique Club.

In 1980 Arthur's son, Alex, took over and expanded the bar to include a grill. Stop by for a great meal and have a look around. It will take you many meals to see everything. Ladies, beware of "Adam" in the ladies' restroom... please don't lift the fig leaf.

Trione's Store

The middle section of the original building that houses Manci's was Trione's Store, owned and operated by Alvira Manci Trione and her son, Leonard "Red" Trione. The store opened in 1903. "Red" Trione is never without a smile. A cornerstone of the community, his good humor is legendary. The store became the central hub of Daphne, serving as not just a grocery store but also the Greyhound bus terminal, an ice cream shop, candy store and florist. A bulletin board on the

Alvira Manci Trione prepares her famous Bega Bread recipe. (courtesy Trione family)

porch served as the source for community announcements, an excellent way to communicate with residents. The store received all of the mail and packages, and had the only telephone in town. The store closed in 1984 and today is occupied by Guido's and Cousin Vinny's, delightful neighborhood restaurants.

Recipe

Bega Bread

An Easter tradition in the family of Helen Trione Callaway. Brought to this country by Helen's grandmother, Carmela Passeri Manci, from her little village in Italy, the tradition was continued by Helen's mother, Alveria Manci Trione, who shared it with her nine children.

"As we grew up, she made some small individual loaves for us, as well as big adult-sized loaves. Sometimes when she sliced it, the children would discover a whole, hard-boiled egg with a colored shell in the middle of the bread loaf. How, we wondered, did that egg get inside the bread," says Helen.

"Traditionally, Bega would be eaten with hard-boiled eggs, Easter ham, and mayonnaise. There was never a written-down recipe for this bread. My mother cooked it as she did everything, with handfuls of this and pinches of that, a feeling of how much was enough.

"I arrived at this recipe from helping and watching my mother through the years."

Ingredients

10 lbs.	plain flour (Gold Medal)
9 pkgs.	yeast (prepared as package suggests and allowed to double in bulk)
3 to 3 1/2 lbs.	grated parmesan cheese (bulk cheese, hand-grated is best)
1 cup	black pepper
3/4 lbs.	Crisco shortening
30	eggs (beaten)
2-3	eggs beaten for brushing tops of the loaves yellow food coloring

Blend flour, cheese and pepper in a large container. Add yeast mixture. Cut in shortening. Add beaten eggs. Mix and knead very well. If more liquid is needed, add lukewarm water. Allow dough to double in bulk. Grease loaf pans thoroughly. Form loaves. Allow loaves to rise. When ready to bake, brush tops of each loaf with beaten egg. Use two or three eggs to make the wash. Recipe makes about 15 loaves (it can be halved). Bake at 350 degrees for 30, 35 or 40 minutes, depending on the size of the loaf. As the Italians say "Mangi benne"!

Manci's watercolor by Christine Linson (courtesy of the artist)

Live Oaks
Gentle Folks

Southern Baptism, *watercolor by Willoweise (courtesy of the artist)*

Live Oaks & Gentle Folks

30

Little Bethel Church, *watercolor by Kellie Mooney (courtesy of the artist)*

Little Bethel Church and Cemetery, 1858

Little Bethel Church was built in 1858 by emancipated slaves on land deeded to them by their ex-master, Major Lewis Stark, who was known for his generosity and integrity. One of the members of the congregation, Russell Dick, was a successful landowner and businessman. He served in the Confederate Army as a cook, and later ran a general store and restaurant on Main Street. He married several times and fathered 23 children.

History records that Russell Dick's mother, Lucy, came to the area on the last voyage of the slave ship, Clothilde. The final resting place for Lucy, Russell Dick and many of his children is the cemetery behind the Little Bethel Church. The church remains a vital part of the community today.

Live Oaks Gentle Folks

Simms Hardware Store, Belforest. Monochrome photo by Kim Pearson.

Sunset Fishermen *oil by Emilee Lyons. (courtesy Sally Lieberman)*

Old Daphne Methodist Church and Cemetery, 1815

On land donated in 1858 by Captain William and Elizabeth Howard, the Old Daphne Methodist Church is the second oldest church in Baldwin County. Of Greek Revival design, it is one of two antebellum churches left in the county. Constructed of heart pine with wooden pegs and random-width floorboards, the original pews and slave gallery have been preserved, as has the black candle-lit chandelier with six globes. Hurricanes of 1906, 1916 and 1979 had damaged the belfry, but it has been rebuilt each time. The original bell, lined with silver dollars, is displayed at the Daphne United Methodist Church.

In 1865, Union soldiers, marching on Spanish Fort, spent the night in the church. The cemetery behind the church houses graves dating back to 1847—many of them unmarked. Casualties from the Civil War are buried here. In 1924, Peter McAdam, a well-known local potter, enclosed his family's plot with clay posts, some of which remain intact today.

Old Daphne Methodist Church and Cemetery.

Sportsman's Marine

Heritage.

Sportsman Marine was started in downtown Fairhope in 1950. Today, we are conveniently located on Highway 98 in Montrose.

Experience.

Sportsman's Marine has delivered over 1,500 boats and 200 outboard motors in the last 10 years, and is one of the top 50 Yamaha dealers in the country.

Service.

Sportsman's Marine has 14 employees with over 128 years of boating experience and serves over 3,000 customers a year.

Commitment.

Sportsman's Marine has been in the business for 53 years with a philosophy to "serve the customer first" and carries a 95 percent customer satisfaction rating.

"Quality of life is so important in today's complicated society. Having our business in Baldwin County not only provides us with great business potential, but the best working environment to make the most of what Baldwin County has to offer.

"From the quality and diverse fishing , recreational boating and water sports to the unparalleled afternoon sunsets, there's no place quite like it." —Hank Miner II, president.

A Montrose canopy of oaks, photo by Charlie Siefried (courtesy First National Bank of Baldwin County)

Live Oaks
Gentle Folks

Bay Mortgage

Alan Luckie knows why so many people decide to locate their homes and recreational residences in Baldwin County, and particularly the Eastern Shore. Alan is a life-long resident, and president of Bay Mortgage, and has seen the Eastern Shore grow and prosper over his professional career as a licensed mortgage broker.

Alan and his staff understand that real estate investments require knowledgeable professionals to assist, both in the purchase of a new home, and with the many financing options available to the homeowner today…whether through FHA, VA or conventional loans.

For more than 15 years, Bay Mortgage has served the Eastern Shore, with a strong commitment to personal, professional service, and a unique understanding of the opportunities, and rewards that come with home ownership in Baldwin County, Alabama. The company has grown 15 fold over the years, and is now recognized as a solid member of the Eastern Shore community.

Alan Luckie also understands the importance of giving back to the community. That's why you will find Bay Mortgage and its employees at the forefront of community activities, and proud sponsor of dozens of community organizations.

"The Eastern Shore is my home," Alan says, "and there's not another place like it this side of heaven!"

Dr. Rockwell

One of Daphne's most beloved physicians and community leaders, Dr. L. E. Rockwell, practiced in the north side of the old McRae Building, at 1880 Main Street for many years. The remainder of this building was a drug store which was originally located on the corner of College and Captain O'Neal Avenue (Dryer's Drug Store).

Dr. Rockwell and his wife Elizabeth reared four sons and one daughter, all of whom have married and live on the Eastern Shore. They have 11 granddaughters. Dr. Rockwell passed away in 1995, leaving his influence on the medical field, Thomas Hospital, public health, the Baldwin County School System, football, the University of Alabama, and every life he came in contact with. He was a true Southern gentleman.

The Rockwell boat, Cindy Sue.

Poem written by Karen Fay Miller in memory of Dr. Rockwell

The Old Country Doctor

*The old country doctor
with a smile in his eyes
held out his hand
to all who came by*

*He delivered our babies
He laid us to rest
He dried all our tears
He gave us his best*

*He healed with love
He gave from the heart
and from his great treasure
we learned as we taught.*

*We will miss you, dear friend
But your life will shine on
in those that you've known
in the work that you've done*

*Now the old country doctor
with a smile in his eyes
looks down from above
as he stands at God's side…*

The Hermit of Montrose

recluse. He took part in the intellectual life of Fairhope and was a well-known, if eccentric, part of the community. As his health failed, he moved back north to be with family, dying at age 88 in 1946 in Oregon.

"For orthodox churches I have little use; I worship God in his own temples. I see him in every bush and every shrub when I walk through the woods." Henry James Stuart, the Hermit of Montrose, lived that philosophy throughout his signature life.

Historic photographs of the Hermit of Montrose and his home. (courtesy Ken Niemeyer)

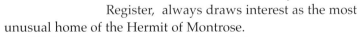

Born in England and a former resident of several Northern states, Stuart moved to Baldwin County in October 1923, when he was 65 years old. He built a one-room, bee-hive house in the woods of Montrose and lived a life of awe-inspiring simplicity. A vegetarian Stuart grew his own food in waist-high planters, weaved rugs on a loom set up in the middle of the house, and slept in a hammock strung up in the middle of the house.

Today the house, added in 1999 to the Baldwin County Historic Register, always draws interest as the most unusual home of the Hermit of Montrose.

While Stuart was known as a hermit, he was not a

Eastern Shore, photo by Charlie Siefried (courtesy First National Bank of Baldwin County)

Live Oaks
Gentle Folks

Original Montrose Post Office.

Montrose Garden Club

Beverly Phillips was the president of the Garden Club in 1951, when the club voted to care for the live oak trees as its project. Miss Beverly, as she was known, the last charter member, died January 8, 2003 at the age of 98, a few months short of her 99th birthday. Today the club has 20 active members, 17 associate members and 4 honorary members.

In 1951, the garden club brought up the discussion of caring for the beautiful oak trees along the streets of Montrose. The Davey Tree Experts gave an estimate of the most urgent work needed and the club members voted to give the first $100 toward the work. Since then the club has continually come up with creative ways to fund the continuing effort to preserve and protect the live oaks of Montrose.

Montrose Post Office

In 1883, Thomas W. Marshall was appointed postmaster of Montrose. He ran a small grocery that included the post office. Following his death in 1890, his wife Ida Marshall was appointed postmaster and a stand-alone post office was built. The small building still stands on Adams Street, where it's been preserved as an important part of Montrose and Baldwin County history.

Coldwell Banker Reehl Properties

Anyone who has ever navigated the potentially confusing waters of buying or selling real estate has quickly discovered what a harrowing experience the process can be. They have also learned the critical importance of having a real estate professional to serve as their own personal pilot guiding them through that intricate procedure. Savvy buyers and sellers today are increasingly coming to rely on the experience and expertise of a professional realtor.

For a decade, thousands of buyers and sellers of residential and commercial real estate along Alabama's Gulf Coast have turned to Coldwell Banker Reehl Properties to provide the peace of mind that comes from working with a proven leader in the industry. Rance Reehl brought more than 10 years experience in new home development and pre-owned residential homes when he began an association with national residential specialist Coldwell Banker in 1993. In just ten years, the company has grown from its original four employees to more than 30 associates and staff today, and will close in excess of $90 million in real estate transactions in 2003. Those sales professionals have vaulted Coldwell Banker Reehl Properties to its position as one of the leading realtors in Mobile and the Eastern Shore communities of Fairhope, Daphne, Point Clear, Montrose, and Spanish Fort.

"The professionalism of our realtors and the personalized service that each gives have been the cornerstone of our success," states Rance Reehl. "We combine this highly personalized service with the latest in cutting edge technology to make buying and selling real estate an enjoyable experience for our clients."

That technology now includes a number of unique and innovative features that Coldwell Banker Reehl Properties clients have come to appreciate. The company's website at www.reehlproperties.com allows one to view all residential and commercial properties that are available in Baldwin County. Photographs and a Virtual Tour gallery highlight many of the homes, offering the prospective buyers the opportunity to shop at home. Another beneficial feature is the carefully selected listing of sub-contractors, suppliers, and service providers in the Concierge Guide which is designed to simplify the buying and selling process creating a "one stop" real estate experience.

That combination of unsurpassed customer service and leading edge technology has resulted in a proven track record. Coldwell Banker Reehl Properties has been designated as one of the premier offices within the Coldwell Banker family nationwide, and consistently ranks among the top five offices in Alabama and is second to none on the Eastern Shore. It has also led to the company's signature appearing on some of the most recognized residential and commercial developments in Baldwin County, such as Chamberlain Trace, a 162-lot residential subdivision; Avalon, a 135-lot residential development; and Daphne Commercial Park. Each has profoundly fueled the real estate climate on the Eastern Shore. It's a safe bet that we'll see that signature on many more developments in the future. — Niki Sepsas

The New Montrose Post Office *watercolor by Coco Hayes (courtesy the artist)*

Montrose

In 1839, Cyrus Sibley secured title to property originally granted to Isabella Narbonne Campbell, along with property adjoining it, platted it and called the area Sibley City.

Cyrus Sibley was born in 1784 in Sutton, Massachusetts. In 1827, he married Eliza Ann Humphries and from that union, nine children were born.

He established a sawmill on Rock Creek to furnish lumber for building. Nothing remains of the old mill, but the site has long been known as the "Old Mill Pond," a favorite spot for fishing.

Mr. Sibley never lived in Sibley City, but most of the property was distributed to his children and other relatives.

In 1856, Mr. Sibley deeded Square No. 12 to be used for school, church and burial place. Records were not kept until 1927, when the Montrose Cemetery Association was formed to take care of the cemetery.

The Montrose Cemetery holds a history of its own with unmarked graves of casualties from the Civil War as well as many generations of residents of the village of Montrose.

Cyrus Sibley can be found within a wrought-iron enclosure on the north east end of the cemetery. Behind his grave stands "The Cottage" home of Julia and Mariah E. Allen and later inhabited by the Jack Oliver Family. Ann Oliver was the great-granddaughter of Mr. Allen. The cottage, also known as the "Gray Cottage," was moved by the Cemetery Association, Montrose Historic Preservation Association and citizens of the community in order to save and preserve the structure.

In 1852 a wharf was built at the foot of Sibley Street. Built by the Steadman Family, mules and ox carts were used to pull goods, coming in by boat, up the steep bluff from the wharf. The wharf was destroyed in the hurricane of 1916. Today you can still see pilings of the original wharf.

Science International Corporation

The Baldwin County education system, along with the county systems in Montgomery and Talladega, have over the years provided a group of graduates who enjoy the art and study of science. Their interest, coupled with studies at institutions of higher learning—Auburn, Huntingdon and Springhill—and years of experience, have created the management team of Science International Corporation.

With its corporate office in Montrose and research laboratories in Daphne, Science International has provided the chemical and process engineering development for companies in Asia, the Americas and Europe. As

a result of Science International research and development over the past decades, pharmaceuticals, plastics and specialty chemicals processes are used worldwide to produce a better life through science.

Live Oaks & Gentle Folks

Jubilee

When it will happen and why, no one really knows! But one thing is for sure; the cry "Jubilee" means excitement, fun and seafood. A steady east wind and a good rain that day are a sure sign a Jubilee is on the way. Jubilees are a rare phenomenon which occur in Bay waters, from Daphne to Point Clear. Daphne shares the distinction of being the "Jubilee City" with only one other place in the world—a remote shore village in India.

Despite the inconvenient hour—jubilees happen at night, often between midnight and dawn—it takes no time for a crowd to gather. And there at the water's edge, stunned and slow-moving is the finest seafood in the world. Flounders, shrimp, crabs and even eels are there for the catching.

There are several theories as to the cause of jubilees. Since rivers feed Mobile Bay, some believe the fish and shellfish may be dazed by a sudden merging of fresh and salt water. Others believe the changing temperature of the water, following heavy rains, causes the phenomenon. Another theory is that tons of dead leaves that are washed into the bay each year deteriorate; a good steady wind and hard rain stir the waters from the bay floor. The oxygen content of the water drops sharply. The sea life is literally breathless, and tries to get air even to the extreme of going ashore.

After the jubilee is over, the work of cleaning your catch brings reality to the fun. However, the end results, the many delicious dishes of fresh seafood, are worth the catch and work!

Jubilee, *photographed by Richard Scardamalia (courtesy of Cynthia Scardamalia-Nelson). At right,* Jubilee, *a watercolor by Jim Gray.*

Live Oaks&
Gentle Folks

Ecor Rouge

The high reddish colored bluffs on the Eastern Shore of Mobile captivated the early European explorers, who reported to their queens and kings about the bluffs that rose over this New World.

Ecor Rouge, French for "Red Bluffs," is the highest point on the coast from Maine to Mexico, at 120 feet above sea level.

The history of the bluffs (along which now lies the residential neighborhood of Montrose) reaches far back into the discovery of the New World.

In 1558 King Phillip of Spain sent an explorer named Guido de las Bazares to select a site for a Spanish colony on Mobile Bay (then called Bahia Filipinia), of which the king had heard so many glowing reports.

Bazares wrote in his records of the site he subsequently chose:

'The Country to the East Side of the bay was much higher than on the west with high red, broken lands.... On which were abundant variety of trees, copious springs and excellent clays for pottery.'

In 1559, Tristan de Luna arrived to attempt to colonize the area Bazares had chosen. He left Vera Cruz on June 11, 1559 with 13 vessels and 1,500 persons, and 250 horses. He made the trip during hurricane season, with loss of lives, horses and goods. Hunger and weather plagued the group for the next six years, until greatly reduced in numbers and strength. Tristan de Luna left the area utterly defeated.

Only crumbling clay-lined storage pits in the vicinity of the Red Bluffs indicated the unsuccessful efforts to colonize what would have been the first permanent European Colony in the New World.

The de Luna Expedition was 60 years before the Pilgrims landed at Plymouth Rock, 143 years before Mobile was founded by the Le Moyne Brothers, and 217 years before the birth of America.

Before Bazares too, Spanish expeditions of Pineda in 1519, Narvaez in 1528 and Maldonada in 1540, all record references to the Red Bluffs.

After the French occupation from 1670 to 1763, the British used Ecor Rouge for a resort. In 1767, engineer Elias Durnford was directed to locate and map out a "healthy" place on the Eastern Shore for the numerous sick soldiers of Fort Charlotte (Mobile). The health resort was to accommodate 250 men. Illness in Mobile had become severe among the British solders. Durnford chose the Ecor Rouge area, for the breezes, fresh water springs, and general pleasantness of the area.

Due to the selection of the site, the population statistics of the Eastern Shore were recorded. In the area were: 17 plantations, 39 white men who could bear arms, 32 Negroes of which 29 were grown men, 21 Negro women and children; a total of 124 souls and 2,280 head of cattle.

The camp was designated "Camp Crofton," which was finished in April 1771. From the time of the early settlements of the Ecor Rouge area, pottery making was popular. The area was and is a natural location for pottery production, since the land, and bluffs themselves, are red clay.

Taken from "A Salute to Baldwin" 1976, page 14, Ecor Rouge: The Red Bluffs.

Page & Palette

As human beings, we are said to be in our prime at thirty-five years of age. Some folks hit their stride earlier, some later—yet to fall into that rhythmic, comfortable gait one must embrace life and all it has to offer. Page & Palette personifies this theory, for at thirty-five, it strides confident and comfortable within a town that has embraced and fed it, much as it has embraced and fed the town of Fairhope.

In critiquing a town, one must survey the loyalty of its inhabitants in their support of local institutions. Fairhope has kept its loyalty localized through its continued patronage of an independent bookstore that, over the years, has become a dear friend to many—at home, as well as abroad. Through this loyal friendship, Page & Palette has managed to stay high and dry amidst a tidal-surge of large, corporate competitors dispersed around its original location in the heart of downtown Fairhope, Alabama.

Hailing from this southern locale, Page & Palette possesses those southern attributes that make this small region of the world such an inviting, comfortable and friendly place. As Southerners, we undeniably feel a certain element of satisfaction in running with "the little guys," for we know them on a more personal level, we have nurtured them and watched them grow. These "little guys" have in return afforded us the opportunity to receive, through a reciprocal relationship, down-to-earth attention to our needs and desires as consumers. There are too few communities left in which individually owned and operated businesses compose the majority of those existing in the area. Page & Palette and Fairhope as a whole has not lost this

Painting by Jo Hart Long (courtesy Karin Wilson).

charming integrity, and hopefully their steadfast commitment will continue on for years to come. The community has grown and progressed, yet it has neither outgrown its appeal to locals nor visitors. Page & Palette is an integral piece of Fairhope's foundation. Through three generations it has prospered, exhibiting its own, as well as its owners, longevity. Now reinvigorated by youthful proprietors, the store is ushered into the future as a mainstay, part of the community's lifeblood. In its lifespan, Page & Palette has undergone a metamorphosis—from bare-bones utility, to its present, modern state of convenience and comfort. Much like the town it calls home, the store has done it all independently, now in a time when independence in any form strikes a more resounding note upon the heart.

I am proud of Page & Palette and would like to thank my family for the energy they have poured into the store as well their dogged commitment to keep its lineage within. Godspeed Page & Palette.

With much love, Joshua Ford Wolff

Fairhope

In 1894, a group of somewhat radical citizens of Des Moines, Iowa decided to settle an experimental city where freedom, fairness and equity ruled. They were dedicated to the Single Tax Theory of philosopher Henry George that calls for common ownership of land, which is leased to individuals for the good of the community. The colony owns 4,000 acres of land that is never sold, but only leased in 99-year terms.

By 1908, there were not enough settlers participating in the colony to incorporate so a city government was created outside the settlers. Since that time, the Single Tax Colony and the city of Fairhope have co-existed.

The colony deeded over 65 acres of parks, including a mile of beach front to the city, on the condition that the property conveyed should be forever used as public parks. A major attraction in Fairhope is the municipal pier and marina. The pier extends 1,366 feet into the bay. The present pier was built in the early 1970s to replace wooden piers which one after the other had been damaged or destroyed in storms and hurricanes.

Water sports, especially boating, are popular in Fairhope. The Fairhope Yacht Club hosts many regattas and is dedicated to enjoying the beauties of Mobile Bay via boat.

The city is a mecca for artists as well as writers. The Eastern Shore Art Center features five galleries and five teaching studios with lots of art work for sale. The gallery is open Monday through Friday, 10 a.m. to 4 p.m. and Saturday 10 a.m. to 2 p.m. The admission is free.

Fairhope Clock, *watercolor by Blanche Sumrall* (courtesy of the artist)

Fairhope Yacht Club, *watercolor by Christine Linson* (courtesy of the artist)

Tomato Lady, *watercolor by Christine Linson* (courtesy of the artist)

Fairhope is listed as one of the top 10 retirement spots by a national publication for senior citizens. Quaint shops and local cuisine attract many visitors. Flowers are a year-round attraction, especially the rose gardens at the municipal pier.

Major events include the Arts & Crafts Festival (founded in 1953) in Fairhope the first weekend in March; the Outdoor Art Show (1973) sponsored by the Eastern Shore Center on the third weekend in March; and the annual Independence Day celebration.

Live Oaks
Gentle Folks

Wolfe Funeral Home

The Lord has blessed our family so graciously. We enjoy life on the Eastern Shore and consider the past 32 years in this community to be one of His greatest blessings. I have been fortunate enough to serve the public as a funeral director for more than 35 years, bringing comfort and quality service to families in their time of need. My wife, Judy, served as a registered nurse for more than 25 years. She is now enjoying working part-time at the funeral home as part of the "family team."

Our daughter, Tina, grew up in the funeral business, as many in the industry have. She has grown to become an integral part of our team, having obtained her funeral director's license.

Gary, Judy and Tina Wolfe.

Gary Simms, general manager, and I have worked together for over 22 years. Glenn Brantley, assistant manager, has worked with us for over 19 years.

Over these years, they and their families have grown to be part of our family. Together we will continue to serve our community with dignity and respect. —Gary Wolfe

Keeping Virgil, *painting by Stacey Howell* (courtesy of the artist)

The Obvious Place

The Obvious Place is the spot where locals and visitors shop for unusual gifts and accessories at affordable prices. Featuring watercolors by Willoweise, the shop is located at 12 North Section Street in Fairhope.

Bay Aviary, *painting by Willoweise* (courtesy of the artist)

The School of Organic Education

The School of Organic Education was founded in 1907 by Marietta Johnson, an innovative educator from Minnesota. Mr. and Mrs. W.S. Comings, good friends of hers who shared her views on education, asked her to come to Fairhope and open a free school. They offered her $25 a month in compensation.

Johnson had visited Fairhope years before and longed to return, so she gladly accepted this opportunity to begin using her newly formed philosophy. She moved to Fairhope with her family and rented a cottage for her school at $15 per month, leaving $10 for salary and supplies. She opened the school with six students and began applying her educational theories.

Marietta Johnson called her method of education "organic" because it follows the natural growth of the child. The program at Fairhope included physical exercise, nature study, music, handwork, field geography, storytelling, fundamental concepts of numbers, drama and games. There were no examinations, grades or report cards given at the school, as Mrs. Johnson wanted her students to enjoy the process of learning as its own reward. "The result of this system," said Mrs. Johnson, "is freedom from self-consciousness, the ability of the child to put all his innate initiative and enthusiasm into his work, the power to indulge his natural desire to learn; thus preserving joy in life and a confidence in himself which frees his energies for work."

Organic School, sculpture by Frances J. Neumann and Barbara Casey, photo by Charlie Siefried (courtesy First National Bank of Baldwin County)

In the next ten years, Marietta Johnson's educational experiment had gained national and international recognition. Her ideal of giving each child the opportunity to develop to his highest capacity without the pressure of competition began to take hold in other schools around the country. Teachers from Oxford, the University of Heidelberg, Harvard, Stanford, Cornell and Dartmouth came to Fairhope to study with Mrs. Johnson. Mrs. Woodrow Wilson invited her to come to Washington to speak, and in 1923, Mrs. Henry Ford donated $13,000 to the school. The famous educator, John Dewey, visited the school and was so favorably impressed that he devoted an entire chapter of his book, *School of Tomorrow*, to the School of Organic Education.

Single Tax Colony Paddlewheeler,
*painting by M. Custee (courtesy of
Elizabeth Rockwell)*

By 1920, there were over 200 students enrolled, many of whom were boarding students. For 32 years, Marietta Johnson served the school, giving all the money made on lecture tours and much of her personal income to the school. When she died in 1938, she had made a profound difference in the lives of a great many people—her students, fellow teachers, friends, and disciples, and her legacy is still alive today.

The original campus was sold in 1988 to Faulkner State Community College for its Fairhope campus, and the bell building has been preserved as a museum and historic monument to Marietta Johnson. The new location of the school is at 8 Marietta Drive in Fairhope. The main building houses the original bell, which is rung at the beginning and end of each school day. Marietta Johnson's philosophy is still the basis of the educational program at the present day School of Organic Education.

Live Oaks
Gentle Folks

Thomas Hospital

In the late 1950's, Mrs. Georganna Thomas Ives donated eight acres of family property to a group of civic-minded visionaries who had formed the Eastern Shore Hospital Board. Their dream was to create a healthcare facility to serve the residents of the Eastern Shore and Baldwin County. On September 6, 1960, that dream became a reality with the opening in Fairhope of Thomas Hospital as an acute-care, non-profit, community hospital with 36 beds and eight general practitioner physicians.

For more than four decades, Thomas Hospital has fulfilled the mission of its founders, and built an enviable reputation for providing quality patient care and compassion in a friendly, hometown environment. Along the way, it has expanded its scope of services and, consequently, its impact on the lives of the county's residents.

The hospital's founders would scarcely recognize the Thomas Hospital of today. The facility, now an integral part of Baldwin County's economy, currently employs more than 900 people and has a volunteer Auxiliary of 400-plus members. The medical staff today includes more than 200 physicians, each committed to providing unsurpassed patient care.

Growth over the years includes a new 100,000 square foot addition to the main hospital in Fairhope. Responding to needs throughout Baldwin County, Thomas Hospital opened an 80,000 square foot outpatient diagnostic and surgery center in Daphne. In 2002, the hospital opened the county's first open heart surgery and balloon angioplasty center.

"We can build new buildings, purchase new technology, and start new programs, but our number one priority will always be patient care," says Owen Bailey, the hospital's president and CEO. "No matter how high tech we become, in a healthcare environment, nothing can take the place of face to face communications and hands-on treatment. Our philosophy at Thomas Hospital is to do everything we do as if we ourselves were the patients. We aim to meet and exceed your expectations, and do so with skill, compassion, sensitivity, and respect."

The board members, staff, employees, and volunteers of Thomas Hospital take very seriously the hospital's role as a leading member of the Baldwin County community. As such, they promote good health in the county through a variety of health education and wellness programs. They also provide a significant amount of charity care, and support local schools, civic groups, and other non-profit organizations. The hospital underscores its commitment to the county's youth through the provision of athletic sponsorships, the Medical Explorers program, and others. Art exhibits promote the healing powers of art, and the hospital was chosen to debut an exhibition of works commemorating the events of September 11, 2001.

Thomas Hospital pledges to continue providing the patient care and professionalism that have resulted in the "Thomas Touch," and sets the hospital apart as a distinctive provider of healthcare services. —Niki Sepsas

Bay Pier, photo by Charlie Siefried (courtesy First National Bank of Baldwin County)

Weeks Bay Estuary

One of the nation's 25 protected reserves, Weeks Bay National Estuarine Research Reserve offers protection to 6,000 acres of coastal wetlands and waterbottoms that provide rich and diverse habitats for fish, crustaceans and shellfish along with many unique and rare plantlife. This estuary, where the rivers meet the sea, is an important scientific research center.

The Weeks Bay Interpretive Center gives visitors the chance to learn about coastal habitats through exhibits, live animal displays, and plants. Guided or self-guided tours of nature trails through wetlands, marshes, bogs, and forests are available at Weeks Bay. The center is located 12 miles east of Fairhope on U.S. 98.

Weeks Bay (monochrome photography by Kim Pearson).

Recipes from Punta Clara Kitchens

Pralines

3 cups	white sugar
1 cup	water
1 tbsp.	butter
1 tsp.	vinegar
3 cups	pecans

Place sugar, water and vinegar in deep pot. Boil to soft ball stage. Add butter and pecans. Continue to cook until syrup spins a light thread. Remove from heat. Cool. Beat until candy holds shape. Drop by spoonfuls on greased waxed paper. Store in airtight container.

Vanilla Fudge

2 cups	sugar
1/2 cup	milk
1 1/2 tbsp.	corn syrup
1/2 stick	oleo
1 cup	pecans

In heavy saucepan mix sugar, milk, corn syrup, vanilla and oleo and cook to 238 degrees, stirring frequently. Cool to 170 degrees, add pecans and beat. When thick pour onto buttered tray. Recipes submitted by Paul Pacey.

The Grand Hotel

Throughout the South, she is known as the "Queen of Southern Resorts." For more than 150 years, this elegant lady has reigned over generations of visitors to Point Clear. Her 300 year old Oak Trees shade footpaths that lead to gracious southern hospitality in a Grand Tradition.

Today, the Grand Hotel Marriott Resort is a 550 acre modern resort, and a luxurious vacation destination with all the amenities families seek, including special programs designed to keep even the most active children entertained.

The Grand Tradition of welcoming guests began in the early 1800's. In 1847, the breathtaking natural beauty of Mobile Bay's Point Clear peninsula inspired a judicious gentleman named F.H. Chamberlain. His vision gave birth to the Point Clear Hotel, a glittering gathering for antebellum Southern society.

The War Between the States ravaged the hotel, but Steamboat Captain H.C. Baldwin rescued the property, and renamed it The Grand in 1875. He used the best wood from

the previous hotels for the heart pine flooring and framing of the main building and doors. The Grand would see subsequent wars. In World War II, it served as a training facility for the U.S. Army Air Force. The building was so revered by the soldiers, they walked the halls in their stocking feet to preserve the pinewood floors for future generations.

The Grand Tradition of hospitality continues today. A recently completed $40 million renovation project transformed the Grand Hotel into a sleek new retreat where elegant, old world touches abound.

New guest rooms have been added, bringing the total to 405, and existing guest rooms have been enhanced as well. An updated ballroom and meeting spaces provide the perfect location for any event. The addition of a 20,000 square foot European Spa complete with indoor swimming pool and fitness facilities, as well as an outdoor swimming pool with waterfall and slide offer a restful respite for any corporate gathering. For those that prefer the feeling of sand between their toes, the bay front beach beckons.

A challenging round of golf can be found at two championship courses that are part of the Grand Hotel Resort. Perry Maxwell, whose other golf course design credits include Southern Hills in Tulsa, Oklahoma, designed the Lakewood Golf Course, built in 1946. At the time it was constructed, Lakewood was considered one of the most prestigious golf clubs in the Southeast. The Azalea course added an additional 18 holes. Both courses received an $8 million makeover that created the most technologically advanced equipment and playing surfaces available.

On any given day during the summer months, the resort offers 14 different family activities, including the Grand Hotel's new $3.5 million, 500,000 gallon water complex. The family pool features a zero entry section for the youngest swimmers, complete with jets and geysers for added fun and surprise.

Mobile Bay's abundant marine life will test the skills of vacationing anglers. Deep sea charters leave right from the Grand Hotel's marina. Sailing, kayaking and a host of other water activities will entice your family to stay a little longer.

For a family boating experience straight out of another century, the schooner Joshua can be chartered. It's a replica of the tall ships that once regularly sailed the waters of Mobile Bay.

Tennis enthusiasts can match their skills with others on any of the ten Rubico surfaced tennis courts. If cycling or jogging is your passion, more than 20 miles of scenic trails await you.

Dining at the Grand has been a tradition for generations. Any meal at the Grand is a treat, but the most talked about meal of the week is the Sunday brunch… a feast for every taste and the signature meal for any visitor to the resort.

Recipe

Crab & Spinach Fondue

1 gal.	Bechamel sauce
4 lbs.	picked claw meat
1/2 cup	Worcestershire sauce
1/2 tsp.	cayenne pepper
2 cups	asaigo shredded
2 cloves	minced garlic
4 ozs.	sherry
2 pkgs.	spinach picked and chopped
2 lbs.	cream cheese
2	anchovy filets
1 cup	minced onion
1 tbsp.	butter

Melt butter in a sauce pot. Add onion, garlic and anchovies. Sweat for 5 minutes and let cool. In a double boiler add bechamel, asaigo and cream cheese. Melt cheese and whisk in spice. Add crabmeat and spinach. Season to taste. Submitted by the Grand Hotel Marriott.

Live Oaks & Gentle Folks

After the Polo Match, *painting by Herman Bischoff* (courtesy of Dr. Albert Corte)

Highland Animal Hospital

Dr. Albert Corte, Jr. has cared for small and large animals since 1969 at The Highland Animal Hospital. Dr. James V. Corte is now a partner in the practice.

First National Bank of Baldwin County

On a peaceful afternoon, when a breeze rustles the branches of a nearby live oak tree, it doesn't take much to figure out why folks love living in Baldwin County.

Simply put, there's just something magical about the place, the land and the people who live here.

Now there's a bank as unique as the people and places it serves-First National Bank of Baldwin County.

You might say "well you had me until you went and compared Baldwin County to a bank, of all things. But, if you're thinking that, then it's pretty clear you're not banking with the folks at First National.

If you were, you would quickly see this bank is as different from the mega-banks based upstate as Baldwin County is different from Jefferson, or Montgomery.

Now you can enjoy the full strength of a nationally chartered bank, without sacrificing the comforts of a hometown institution.

When you call our office, the phone actually rings in the city you dialed-not Birmingham or Montgomery (as it does for at least three other banks).

Call and talk to a banker who saw the same sunrise you did.

Bring your questions to someone who's lived here long enough to see a sapling become a mighty source of shade.

Know a bank that is open early, open late, and open-minded.

A bank that, like you, knows why we're here.

And all you have to do to begin enjoying the pleasures and rewards of banking with First National is to call any of our three offices in Foley, Gulf Shores, or Fairhope. In Fairhope, the number is 990-6474. You'll even be able to talk to a real human who lives on the Eastern Shore.

First National Bank of Baldwin County. One more reason to be glad you live here.

Loxley

John Edward Loxley was born in London, Ontario, Canada in 1841. Upon moving to Michigan, he met and married Mary Jeanette Cameron and had three children. In 1863, Loxley mustered into service with Company T, First Regiment Michigan Engineers and Mechanics. Two years later he was wounded in battle and was given an honorable discharge. By virtue of his service in the Civil War he became a U.S. citizen.

At the turn of the century (1900) John Loxley established a lumber camp in a small village in Baldwin County named Bennet. The town was later called Loxley.

A large number of men followed Mr. Loxley and a lumber camp that included a commissary and a sawmill was built. A railroad was opened in 1906 and was called the Fort Morgan Line. The only roads were wagon roads to Bay Minette. In 1920 other business such as an egg store, train depot, telegraph office, land office, bank, butcher shop, grocery store, post office, cement block plant, a blacksmith and feed store were established.

In addition to the timber business, the process of extracting rosin from the pine trees was a big business with the Barnhill Turpentine Still being one of the largest.

{The Strawberry Festival (since 1988) is celebrated in Loxley the first Saturday in May.}

Loxley has been called the "Trucking Mecca" with its location just off Interstate 10, where you will find several large truck stops.

Loxley, like other parts of Baldwin County, it is an agriculture area and is also well suited for cattle growing. Strawberries are a big spring crop. There is a large plant-growing nursery located near I-10 convenient for trucking. You will find many farmers markets that sell fresh grown vegetables and fruits. Don't miss the herb store.

Summerdale

By 1905, 43 Polish families had migrated to Summerdale, the town said to be named for the Eli Summer's Farm. Potatoes were an early crop, stored in potato sheds built along the railroad that ran through the center of town. Trains were used to move the potatoes to market.

The railroad was removed in the early 1980s and the last of the potato sheds have only recently been taken down.

In 1918, tobacco was grown as an experimental crop sold to the Alabama Tobacco Company. Soon the town had developed an extensive business in growing and curing cigar tobacco. Large barns used to store and dry tobacco dotted the landscape.

The Old Tobacco Warehouse, now owned by B. J. Blanchard, houses a golf museum—open by appointment only. Blanchard has spent 35 years collecting golf memorabilia, including golf clubs and tennis racquets used by the famous female athlete, Babe Didrikson Zaharias.

Migrant Worker's Child, *watercolor by Hazel Lowery* (courtesy of Annette and Jim Lay)

Recipes

Greg's Favorite Strawberry Pie

1 pkg.	8 oz. cream cheese, softened
8 oz.	whipped topping
1	graham cracker crust
1 cup	confectioners sugar
2 cups	(or more) chopped Burris grown strawberries

Mix cream cheese and confectioners sugar; add whipped topping and strawberries and mix well by hand. Put in crust and garnish with strawberries. Chill.

Miss Kay's Favorite Peach Pie

5 cups	sliced fresh Burris grown peaches
1	unbaked 9-inch pastry shell
1/3 cup	butter, melted
1 cup	sugar
1/3 cup	all-purpose flour
1	egg

Place peaches in pastry shell. Combine remaining ingredients, and pour over peaches. Bake at 350 degrees for one hour and 10 minutes.

Apricot Punch

3	large cans apricots
3 doz.	lemons, juiced
1 bottle ginger ale	
3	oranges, sliced thin into punch bowl

Puree apricots in blender, add lemon juice, add water to dilute and sugar to taste. Chill thoroughly. When ready to serve add ginger ale and ice ring. Submitted by Cecile Thompson Barnhill

Divinity Candy

2 cups	sugar
1/3 cup	corn syrup
1/3 cup	water
2	egg whites
1 cup	chopped pecans

Mix sugar, syrup and water. Cook until it will spin a thread. Pour 1/2 into beaten egg whites slowly beating all the while. Cook the other half until a drop forms a hard ball when dropped in cold water. Then pour into first half and beat until creamy. Add nuts. Drop by teaspoonfuls into waxed paper to cool. Submitted by Cecile Thompson Barnhill

Irish Coffee Cake

Cream together:
1/2 cup	butter
1 cup	white sugar

Add:
2	eggs, one at a time and mix well

Sift together:
2 cups	plain flour
1 tsp.	baking powder
1 tsp.	soda
1/2 tsp.	salt

Add alternately with:
1 cup	sour cream

1 tsp. vanilla

Nut mixture:

1/3 cup brown sugar

1/4 cup white sugar

1 tsp.   cinnamon

1 cup   chopped pecans

Mix all ingredients together. Pour half of batter into 9 x 13 inch lightly greased pan. Sprinkle with 1/2 of nut mixture. Spread remaining batter over nut mixture and top with rest of nut mixture. Bake 40 to 45 minutes in a 325 degree oven. Submitted by Jean Fontaine, Silverhill

Potato Cheese Croquettes

2 cups   cold mashed potatoes

1   egg

          salt to taste

1 cup   grated cheddar cheese

3/4 tsp. Accent

1/2 cup   fine dry bread crumbs

1/2 cup   milk

Break up potatoes. Beat egg until frothy, add potato pieces gradually, beating until blended. Stir in cheese and seasonings. Shape as desired. Dip into crumbs. Fry in shallow hot fat until brown. Makes 4 to 6 servings. Submitted by Jean Fontaine, Silverhill

Burris Sporting Art Gallery

Greg and Kay Burris, owners of Burris Farm Market, opened the "sporting art gallery for the serious collector" in December 1999. The house with the big fish out front contains paintings, etchings,  drawings, sculpture and prints with hunting, fishing and wildlife themes. The gallery also carries duck decoys, antique fishing lures and collectible tackle.

The gallery is a long-time dream of Greg Burris who had the old tenant farm house (built in 1883) moved from a location 12 miles away. The building was renovated over a period of several years preserving the basic layout of the house, saving the original wood and paint as much as possible.

Many of the decoys offered for sale are from Greg's collection that he started many years ago. The same is true of many of the approximately 1,000 fishing lures. Some of the duck decoys date back to early 1900. Many visitors from other parts of the country are astonished to see so many such items together in one location. The gallery is unique and very likely the only one of its kind in the region.

The artwork in the gallery is by nationally known artists and local favorites.

Magnolia Plantation, Loxley, *watercolor by Barbara Tonsmeire (courtesy Annette and Jim Lay)*

Good Scents Herbs and Flowers

A second generation family business, Good Scents Herbs and Flowers was known when founded in 1976 as Succulent World by Jim and Linda Monroe. In July 1999, they sold the business to their daughter, Lorraine, and her husband, Michael Keane.

The name was changed to better reflect the family's belief about the many good scents to be found here, as well as the good sense it makes to be organic and natural—especially in the foods we eat. Their beautiful herbs and flowers are grown in the most natural way with no special or hard to repeat growing conditions.

The company can offer the best advice on growing herbs on the gulf coast, with an outstanding culinary herb collection with many different and fragrant scents and flavors.

Fall, winter and through to the spring, the lettuce and salad greens are luscious, with plenty of varieties from which to choose. From arugula to radicchio to edible flowers, you will delight in all of the flavors and colors. In the spring you'll find a great selection of heirloom tomatoes and vegetables.

All plants are selected with the Deep South in mind—growing only what best tolerates hot humid summers and mild winters. Winter is by the way the best time to start most perennial herbs and lettuce gardens.

Around Valentine's Day you can find the flowers of early spring, such as sweet peas, bachelor's buttons, larkspur, violas and many old-fashioned and fragrant flowers. All of these lovely flowers are ready to plant outside because they have grown all winter in unheated cool greenhouses. They are tough, hardened and ready to go.

The store is open Monday through Saturday, 9 to 5, and Sundays in early spring through summer.

Robertsdale clock, photo by Charlie Siefried (courtesy First National Bank of Baldwin County)

Robertsdale

Located in the heart of Baldwin County, Robertsdale is known as "The Hub City." Robertsdale was founded in 1905 by the Southern Plantation Corporation of Chicago, Illinois and named after one of its officials, Dr. B. F. Roberts. The founder was attracted to this location by the L&N Railroad, which had recently been extended to Foley. The Town was incorporated in 1921.

The town is the annual host of the Baldwin County Fair, held each fall. It was started as a calf show in the late 1940s. Arts and crafts, traditional fair rides, cooking and cattle shows are part of the festival.

Since the 1940s, the Robertsdale Livestock Auction has held auctions every Monday and is one of the few auctions remaining in the Southeastern United States.

If you find yourself in Robertsdale at lunchtime, stop by Mama Lou's for the best buffet in town.

Recipes

Sauerkraut Soup

4 1/2 cups	water
4 medium	potatoes, peeled and cubed
1/2 tsp.	salt
1/2 pkg.	smoked sausage links, cut up
1 16 oz. can	sauerkraut
1 medium	onion chopped
1 clove	minced garlic
1/4 tsp.	caraway seed
1 tbsp.	fresh dill finely chopped
1 cup	sour cream
1 tbsp.	flour

Bring water, potatoes and salt to boil in heavy pot. Cook until tender. Add sausage, undrained sauerkraut, onion, garlic, dill and caraway seed, bringing to a boil. Meanwhile in a small bowl combine sour cream and flour. Gradually stir in 1 cup hot mixture into sour cream mix. Add to big pot. Heat well but do not boil. Season with salt and pepper.
Submitted by Aina Olson Swoboda

Poppy Seed Cake

4	eggs
2 cups	sugar
12 oz.	container poppy seed filling
1 1/2 cps.	vegetable oil
3 cups	flour
1/2 tsp.	baking soda
1 lg.	can evaporated milk
1/2 cup	pecans, chopped
	confectioners sugar

Cream eggs with sugar; add poppy seed filling and oil. Sift flour with soda and add alternately with milk to eggs. Fold in pecans. Bake in ungreased 10 inch tube pan for one hour and 10 minutes at 350 degrees. Cool and sprinkle with confectioners sugar. Submitted by Georgia Snazel Kucera

Kolaches (Little Batch)

1/4 cup	sugar
1/2 cup	Crisco
1 tsp.	salt
1 pkg.	dry yeast
1/2 cup	warm milk or water
1	egg
3 cups	all purpose flour

Add 1/2 cup boiling water or milk to Crisco. Let stand until lukewarm. Beat 1 egg, add to yeast, and cooled Crisco mixture. Add 3 cups flour and mix until it has a shiny look. Let rise for 1 hour; then cut out by tablespoon and roll into balls and let rise. Fill with your favorite fruit filling. Prune filling or fig preserves suggested. Sprinkle with powdered sugar.
Submitted by Georgia Snazel Kucera

Still Life, *watercolor by Jo Patton (courtesy of Sally Lieberman)*

Minimac Wildflower Bog

Surrounding a five-acre lake and honey-combed with walking paths, the Minimac Wildflower Bog allows visitors to see the many varieties of wildflowers native to Southern bogs. The hillside leading to the lake is carpeted with rare and unusual wildflowers.

The Minimac Wildflower Bog is privately owned and preserved for the enjoyment of plant lovers and wildflower enthusiasts. From early April through September, you can find acres of rare flowers, including the carnivorous pitcher plant and the colorful nodding flower. The seasons bring glorious changes to the bog, from rare orchids to the colorful red bloom of the Southern pine lily and the golden hues of the goldcrest.

Live Oaks & Gentle Folks

Wooden Bowls Turned from Fallen Wood, *by Dr. John B. Howell*

Recipes

God's Favos (Bozi Milosti) Czech

2   eggs slightly beaten
2 cups   plain flour
2 tbsp.   cream (sweet or sour)
2 tbsp.   rum
1 tsp.   salt

Mix eggs with cream and rum. Add to flour and salt, stirring and kneading on floured board until smooth. Roll out thin as noodles, cut in diamond shapes 3 x 3. Make two 1-inch slits in middle of each piece and fry in deep fat on both sides. Remove to unglazed paper and sprinkle with powdered sugar. Submitted by Helen Mazel Douglas

Meringue Kisses (Pusinky) Czech

3   egg whites
1 cup   confectioners sugar
1/2 tsp. cream of tartar
            pinch of salt

To egg whites, add salt and cream of tartar and beat until stiff. Add 3/4 cup of sugar gradually. Continue beating until very heavy. Fold in remaining 1/4 cup sugar, mixing well without beating. With teaspoon or using pastry bag shape small meringues on greased and floured baking sheet. Dry rather than bake them at 250 degrees for 2 hours. Meringues must stay dry and white. Submitted by Helen Mazel Douglas

Czechoslovakian Cabbage Soup

2 lbs.   beef soup bones
1 cup   chopped onions
3   carrots, peeled and chopped
2 cloves garlic chopped
1   bay leaf
2 lbs   beef short ribs
1 tsp.   dried leaf thyme
1/2 tsp. paprika
8 cups   water
8 cups   coarsely chopped cabbage
2 cans   tomatoes (16 oz.)
2 tsp.   salt
1/2 tsp. tabasco sauce
1/4 cup   chopped parsley
3 tbsp.   lemon juice
3 tbsp.   sugar
1 can   sauerkraut (16 oz.)

Place beef bones, onions, carrots, garlic and bay leaf in roasting pan. Top with short ribs; sprinkle with thyme and paprika. Roast, uncovered in 450 degree oven for 20 to 30 minutes or until beef is browned. Transfer meat and vegetables into large kettle. Add water, cabbage, tomatoes, salt and Tabasco. Bring to boil. Cover and simmer one to one and half hours. Skim off fat. Add parsley, lemon juice, sugar and sauerkraut. Cook uncovered for one hour. Remove bones and ribs from kettle. Cool and remove meat from bones and return to kettle. Cook five minutes. Yield 12 servings.
Submitted by Aina Olson Swoboda

Live Oaks Gentle Folks

Lutheran Zion Church, *watercolor by Tom Roberts (courtesy of the artist)*

Silverhill

Silverhill, a small quaint town was settled in 1896 by Scandinavians, led by Oscar Johnson. The site was chosen for its natural beauty, high altitude, and climate beneficial for good health. It is still unsure how the name Silverhill came about. Some say that in the early history of the town, laborers at the turpentine still had to climb the "hill" to get their weekly pay in silver coins. Thus the name became "Silverhill." In the first year of its existence, the community was quarantined for yellow fever.

The original families were primarily Swedes, Norwegians and Danes from Illinois, Wisconsin, and Minnesota. Later Bohemians, Yugoslavs and Czechoslovakians joined them.

In 1908, Woodhaven Dairy, one of Baldwin's first cream-eries, was opened in Silverhill. Other farms grew large vegetable crops. Early records show that the pioneers had trouble with wild razorback hogs, which were left by Desoto. The fierce and hungry animals invaded picnics and had to be run back into the woods.

T.A. Johnson built the People's Supply Store in 1902, and it carried food from Scandinavian homelands. Customers could find such treats as dried cod and Carraway cheese. Today People's Supply houses United Bank. Some of the first structures built in Silverhill were churches. The First Sweden Baptist Church was founded in 1899 and services were conducted in Swedish until 1930. The Lutheran Zion Church was organized in 1905 and conducted services in Swedish until 1919.

In 1922, the Pouchy Zabavni Krouzek Hall, known today as the PZK Hall, was built to provide a social gathering place for Czechoslovakians. The Silverhill Library was built in 1896 and is still in use today.

The Silverhill Heritage Day Festival is celebrated the first Saturday in September.

Silverhill Library, *watercolor by Tom Roberts (courtesy of the artist)*

Live Oaks Gentle Folks

Live oak in silhouette, photo by Charlie Siefried (courtesy First National Bank of Baldwin County)

Live Oaks &
Gentle Folks

(South Baldwin)

Foley

Foley was founded in 1901 by J.B. Foley, a drug manufacturer and Republican Party leader from Chicago. Mr. Foley was affectionately called the "Pine Tar and Honey Man" for his cough remedies. He founded the Magnolia Land Company and purchased over 50,000 acres in south Baldwin.

In 1904, to ensure the growth of the town, the L & N Railroad was extended to Foley from Bay Minette. Originally the rail was to run to Fort Morgan, but the hurricane of 1906 devastated the area and plans to finish the track were dropped.

By 1905 Foley had a post office, saloon, livery stable and L & N rail station. The city served as the agricultural marketing center for south Baldwin and the L & N line shipped produce all over the South.

Foley was incorporated in 1911. In 1920 the Delco plant developed into the present Riviera Utilities, a large private utility company that still serves south Baldwin and the Eastern Shore. The Ward Snook Family took over a defunct telephone company, which was later called Gulf Telephone.

World War II brought the installation of Brian Field, a branch of the Pensacola Naval Base Training Facility.

The Magnolia Hotel, Foley's oldest existing structure, was built in 1908 by the Magnolia Land

Foley Depot, watercolor by Blanche Sumrall (courtesy of the artist)

Company to house tourists who came looking to settle in the area. John Snook later bought the hotel.

Foley, known as the Forward City, has indeed moved forward to become the main seat of commerce, a manufacturing and transportation hub, and a destination for tourists and shoppers from throughout the nation.

Highway 59 runs through the center of Foley by the Riviera Center, the most popular shopping area in Baldwin County. Truly there you can "shop till you drop."

Foley Mayor Tim Russell is a wealth of Baldwin County knowledge and a true Southern gentleman. The city hosts Art in the Park, the second weekend in May.

City of Foley Depot and Museum

First built in 1905, the Louisville and Nashville Railroad came to Foley. Two trains a day ran between Foley and Bay Minette, wood-burning engines carrying passengers and freight through Baldwin County. The original depot in Foley burned in 1908. It was rebuilt and served as a community hub for decades. When the L & N discontinued service, the depot was dismantled and moved to Magnolia Springs. In the early 1990s, the depot was deeded back to the city of Foley. Renovations were begun to recreate the depot and turn the facility into a historical museum.

Craft Farms

The Craft Farms Golf Resort of today originated as a gladiolus farm founded by R.C. Craft. In 1963 Craft started his own company by purchasing 20 acres of gladiolus. Looking for a business that could be profitable year-round, Craft discontinued the gladiolus in 1975 to focus on corn and soybeans. That same year, his son Robert and his wife Beth created a successful sod business that now has been in operation for nearly 30 years.

In the late '80s, the Crafts were looking to diversify by building a golf course. They had the land and the grass, and with perseverance, were able to convince Arnold Palmer to help them build their facility. The Cotton Creek Club opened its first 18 holes in 1988. Palmer followed-up and turned Cotton Creek into a 27-

hole course in 1992. In 1997, 9 more holes were added to make-up the new Cypress Bend course. Senior PGA player Larry Nelson designed the Woodlands at Craft Farms.

Craft Farms Coastal Golf Resort is home to 54 holes of golf. In addition to a turf farm and three courses, Craft Farms has 300 members, two Clubhouses, full-service golf shops, meeting facilities and is home to the world-renowned McCollough Institute for Appearance and Health. The Craft Farms community of 400 homes is nestled among Cotton Creek and Cypress Bend and shares the property with the on-site Cypress Point condominiums and the Courtyard by Marriott. Craft Farms is proud to have taken a major role in the development of the area's tourism industry and is especially excited about the future of the Alabama Gulf Coast.

Live Oaks Gentle Folks

The Magnolia Hotel

From the time the rail depot was built along the L&N Railroad line in Foley in 1905, it was inevitable that a hotel would soon follow. The Magnolia Hotel dates from 1908, when it opened as a simple hotel and boarding house. Through the decades and various owners, the hotel has stood the test of time. These days it is being renovated and restored as a bed and breakfast.

Some of the architectural treasures inside the hotel include an 1890 Waterford crystal chandelier, an early Victorian bed made of solid walnut, a Jenny Lynn spool rope bed, cedar-lined closets, ballroom chandeliers of crystal and 24k gold, and an Austrian straw-burner porcelain heater dating to the 1850s.

Holmes Medical Museum

The Holmes Medical Museum is located on the second floor of the Stelk/Crosby building at the southwest corner of Laurel Avenue and McKenzie Street in Foley. The building was originally constructed in 1906 as a hardware store; the upper story served as a private residence. In 1916, the upper story of this building became the office of Dr. Sibley Holmes.

In 1928, Dr. W.C. Holmes joined his father in the medical practice. Both doctors dreamed of opening a hospital to serve South Baldwin County. Their dream was realized in 1936 when the Sibley Holmes Memorial Hospital opened; sadly the elder Dr. Holmes died before the hospital opened. The hospital remained in operation until 1958 when South Baldwin Hospital opened.

The only public hospital in Baldwin County that predates World War II, the hospital has survived as the Holmes Medical Museum, open Monday through Friday, 10 a.m. to 4 p.m. No admission fee is charged. Visitors can see the original operating room, recovery room and period autoclave and sterilizer.

Baldwin Mutual Insurance

From an inauspicious birth as the incorporation in 1921 of 20 south Alabama farmers into their own insurance company, Baldwin Mutual has grown to become one of the state's premier names in property and casualty insurance. In fact, the company is Alabama's only true mutual property casualty company insuring both property and casualty. The company's original single employee and lone agent have over the course of the last eight decades grown to an organization of 38 employees and more than 300 agents. Each is committed to maintaining the high standards and the principles on which the organization was founded: providing the finest insurance products available to its mutual policyholders at the most reasonable price possible.

Baldwin Mutual offers a wide range of quality insurance products to cover homes, farms, equipment, mobile homes, and other property. The company's competitive rates and emphasis on customer service have been largely responsible for its consistent growth.

"Being a true mutual company is what sets us apart from other insurers," states Tim Russell, Baldwin Mutual's president and CEO and the mayor of Foley, Alabama. "As a mutual company, our policyholders have a vested interest in Baldwin Mutual as they are the owners of the company. And, unlike many companies who do business in Alabama but are headquartered elsewhere, we are based in this state. Insurance premiums paid by our policyholders remain in Alabama, and are re-invested in this state. We have a substantial investment in Alabama, and are proud to call it our home."

While the company was founded in Baldwin County and continues to bear its name, Baldwin Mutual has experienced considerable geographic as well as corporate expansion over the course of its existence. The company underwrites policies statewide, and maintains offices in Mobile, Birmingham, and Florence. Baldwin Mutual agents across Alabama have insured thousands of policyholders ranging from small businesses and industries to farms and homeowners.

The personal service and "hometown" atmosphere that have come to identify Baldwin Mutual become evident with the first handshake between the policyholder and the agent. These representatives of the company strive to build lasting relationships with their clients. Agents and adjusters are also neighbors, and are just a phone call away. And since Baldwin Mutual handles all of its own claims in-house, policyholders are assured of prompt, attentive service from adjusters, often visiting the client the same day a claim is made.

The professionals at Baldwin Mutual believe that the creation of a "hometown" atmosphere involves being a good corporate citizen of that hometown. Putting that philosophy into practice, the company remains closely involved in the activities of the South Baldwin Chamber of Commerce, the U.S. Chamber of Commerce, and the Business Council of Alabama. — Niki Sepsas

Riviera Utilities

Providing high quality reliable service to customers at reasonable rates, Riviera Utilities is committed to constantly improving both the company and the communities it serves.

Headquartered in the city of Foley, Riviera Utilities serves customers within the corporate limits of the city with electrical, water, wastewater, natural gas and cable television services. A branch office in the City of Daphne provides electrical service to Daphne, Point Clear, Spanish Fort, and portions of Fairhope. The utility, overseen by general manager and governed by a five member board of directors, also serves the municipalities of Bon Secour, Daphne, Elberta, Gulf Shores, Lillian, Loxley, Magnolia Springs, Robertsdale, and Summerdale.

The history of Riviera Utilities is tied inextricably to the economic development and growth of Baldwin County. On October 2, 1916, the Town of Foley entered into an agreement with Swanstrom Brothers Saw Mill to install 12 50-watt street lights for $60 and to furnish current at the rate of $15 per month. The street lighting installation was completed during the month of December and Foley paid its first electric bill January 2, 1917. This was the beginning of public utility service in Foley.

Following those humble beginnings, a number of public and private entities developed the city's utility system. Riviera Utilities Corporation was formed on February 10, 1929 by Central States Edison Company, then owner of the former Foley Light & Power Company.

Later, in 1951, the Alabama Legislature enacted a law

which allows municipalities to create an incorporated utilities board for the purpose of owning, operating and improving an electric system, natural gas system, water works system, and a sanitary sewer system. Pursuant to that law, the Town of Foley established its Utilities Board on May 30, 1952.

This new board acquired the electric system and assets of the Foley Municipal Electric Utilities Board on July 1, 1952, as well as the water system and portions of the sanitary sewer system which were owned by the Town of Foley.

In 1956, the State Legislature increased the size of the utilities board of directors from three members to five, all of whom must be qualified electors of the City of Foley.

Presently, the Board of Directors has the following members: R. Timothy Russell, Mayor of the City of Foley, Samuel F. Parker, Jr., Vice-Chairman, Arthur A. Holk, Charles J. Ebert, Jr., Council Member of the City of Foley, and Robert M. Davis. Mike Dugger is general manager.

German Recipes

Chicken Schnitzel

4	boneless chicken breasts
1/2 tsp.	salt
1/4 tsp.	sugar
3/4 cup	fine dry bread crumbs
1 tbsp.	chopped parsley
2	eggs
2 tbsp.	water
1/2 cup	flour
3 tbsp.	butter
3 tbsp.	corn oil
	grated rind of 1 lemon

Pound chicken to 1/2 inch thickness. Stir together bread crumbs, parsley and lemon rind in a dish. In another dish, lightly beat eggs and water and place flour in another dish. Coat each piece of chicken lightly with flour, then egg, then bread crumbs. Shake off excess and chill at least 15 minutes or up to 2 hours.
Heat 1 1/2 tablespoons of butter and 1 1/2 tablespoons oil in large skillet. Cook chicken over medium high heat until browned and done.

German Sour Cream Twists

3 1/2 cps.	flour
1 tsp.	salt
1 cup	butter
1 pkg.	dry yeast softened in a 1/4 cup warm water
1/4 cup	thick sour cream
1	whole egg
2	egg yolks
1 tsp.	vanilla
1 cup	sugar (for rolling)

Sift flour and salt in a bowl. Cut in shortening. Dissolve yeast in water and add to flour and salt along with sour cream, eggs and vanilla. Mix well, cover with damp cloth and refrigerate 2 hours. Roll half the dough on sugared board to about 8 x 16 inches. Fold ends toward center, ends overlapping. Sprinkle with sugar, roll again. Repeat third time. Roll about 1/4 inch thick. Cut into strips 1 x 4 inches. Twist ends in opposing directions, horseshoe shape. Bake at 375 degrees for 15 minutes.

Recipes submitted by Anna Marie Manley

Southern Petals

Travel down Highway 98 to Elberta to visit a small, quaint, yellow shop that houses Southern Petals. Gary and Sherry Peaden, along with their six children, started growing flowers to harvest and sell. The shop is open all year, but fresh flowers are available only during the summer months. At the height of the season, the family picks about 3,000 flowers a week.

The flowers are sold in brightly painted cans and mason jars. An honor box is the only cashier.

Elberta

The Baldwin County Colonization Company founded the town of Elberta in 1904. One of the German founders from Chicago named the town after the Elberta peach, one of his favorites. The new town's 53,000 acres of land were purchased from the Southern States Lumber Company. The town did not grow haphazardly; its founders methodically laid it out so that the neat, even blocks were bordered on all

Farm field, photo by Charlie Siefried (courtesy First National Bank of Baldwin County)

four sides by streets. One-room schoolhouses were built every two to four miles.

The early crops were Irish potato, sweet potato and sweet corn. A story is told that one immigrant came to raise pineapples from pine trees. He bought his land on the strength of photos of pinecones purported to be pineapples.

More than 60 dialects from Europe, Asia and the Arctic Circle were spoken in this remote town, which even today, calls itself the "Town of Friendship."

Elberta is well known for its "Sausage Festival," held in March and October, where the main attraction is—you guessed it—German sausage! The St. Benedict German Festival is held in April.

Live Oaks & Gentle Folks

Sweet Home Farm

A working family dairy established in 1985, Sweet Home Farm is the first licensed farmstead cheesemaker in Alabama. A small mom and pop operation, Sweet Home Farm handcrafts a wide variety of cheeses. All cheese is made from fresh milk from the farm's Guernsey cows, culture, salt and enzymes and aged for a minimum of 60 days. Using a variety of sustainable agricultural practices permits quality control as cows produce milk that is then transformed into cheese. No herbicides, pesticides or growth hormones are used on the farm, and no preservatives or coloring find their way into Sweet Home Farm cheeses. The cheese is sold exclusively at the farm's store.

Varieties of cheeses sold include Elberta, Bama Jack, Gouda, Feta, Montabella, Baldwin Swiss, Cheese Fudge, Blue, Pepato Asiago, and Romano.

Live oak, photo by Charlie Siefried (courtesy First National Bank of Baldwin County)

Biophilia Nature Center

A native plant nursery and bookstore, the Biophilia Nature Center features insect-eating plants, from Venus fly traps to pitcher plants to butterflies in all their life stages to other native wildlife. Since 1991, biologist Carol Lovell-Saas, architect Fred Saas and volunteers have worked to restore the swamp, pitcher plant bog, forests and wildflower meadows at the 20-acre nature center. Here you'll find hundreds of native species along with a library, book store and gift shop. The center is open from 9 a.m. to 4 p.m. five days a week.

Lillian

In 1763, King Charles III of Spain issued land grants to settlers along Perdido Bay, provided they were Catholic and had farmed three good crops in a row. Three brothers by the name of Suarez were given a tract of land that stretched from the Perdido River to Mobile Bay. This area was rich in virgin timber so the timber became very important.

Fishing and farming helped to sustain the settlement. The Old Spanish Cemetery gate has written on it; "The King of Spain gave us our grants, the bay gave us our bread." Many of the early settlers are buried in this private plot which is nes-tled in the newly developed subdivision of Spanish Cove. Some of the early families were Suarez, Resmondo, Fell, Donaldson, Scott and Kee.

The Resmondo Family came from Venice, Italy in the early 1800s and established a business building wooden fishing boats. Today, still on Palmetto Creek, the family builds wooden boats as well as large fiberglass charter fishing boats.

Mary Scott, whose family has lived in the area for generations, (her father was Mr. Fred M. Scott) married Berkeley Smith, who was a descendent of the Fell and Resmomdo family. She tells a story of a very well-to-do resident John Innerary. It seemed when he would be gone for a spell, pirates would attack ships in the Gulf. When he would come back, he would be richer than when he left. It was also believed Jean LaFitte came to this area after he was run out of New Orleans. As time passed and ships kept being pirated, it was believed John Innerary and Jean LaFitte were one and the same. It has always been rumored that pirates buried treasure on the shores of the Perdido Bay. Many a person has looked for these treasures over the years.

The town was named Lillian for the daughter of the first postmaster, William Kee in 1884. In addition to Perdido Bay, there are many waterways in this area, such as Palmetto Creek and Soldier Creek named for an encampment of soldiers during the civil war.

Today many of the residents are retirees who enjoy this quiet and relaxed area's fishing and water sports.

The Finding Of Perdido

A puff came out of the Westward-
A Flurry- the waves went dead.
The moon broke through the flying clouds
And we saw the shore ahead.

Sand-dune following sand–dune
And just one tiny rift,
So we headed foe that through the breakers.
Sail lowered, we let her drift.

We landed at last on an island-
Island we called Ono.
And slept the night on her beaches-
Beaches whiter than snow.

Next morning we followed the channel,
Twisting and winding and slow,
Creeping around our island-
Curious where it would go.

The water was clear and tranquil,
The shores were wooded and high.
And we felt a growing calmness
As point after point crept by.

And so we came into Perdido-
The Bay that was lost and found,
Where human troubles grow dim and fade
And nerves forget to pound.

High bluffs breaking the sky-line,
Pine flats and cedar and oak-
And we knew we had found our stopping place
Tho' not a man of us spoke.

Thus was Perdido settled,
On its shores each built his shed,
And the king of Spain gave us our grants
And the Bay gave us our bread.

-Fred M. Scott

Moore Brothers Village Market & Jesse's Restaurant

Time may not have actually stood still in historic Magnolia Springs, but it has definitely moved at a much slower pace than in the rest of the world. Perhaps it's because of the languid river that meanders lazily through town past the moss-draped live oak trees that create this picture postcard setting in Baldwin County. Many feel that a major reason is one man's effort to preserve a piece of the town's history—a charming reminder of a bygone era.

Charles Houser grew up in Magnolia Springs, and lists among his earliest memories the daily visits he made to the Moore Brothers General Merchandise store. Opened in 1922 by brothers Mack and Gary Moore, the store not only supplied the residents of Magnolia Springs with everything from socks and hardware to groceries and fishing tackle, but also doubled as the place where locals met to swap news and gossip.

The adjacent post office featured the only full-time river mail delivery in the United States. The store's closing in 1993 signaled the end of a colorful chapter in the town's history.

In 1998, Houser returned to his boyhood hometown with a dream to re-open the old store and infuse into it the same nostalgic charm that had identified it for 71 years. He has done that and more. Re-named the Moore Brothers Village Market, the store is once again a place where locals gather in an atmosphere reminiscent of a Norman Rockwell painting. Noticeably absent are the mountains of pre-packaged foods of the sprawling super centers.

The Market, now on the National List of Historic Places, features a full selection of groceries, wines, cheeses, a deli, and freshly cut USDA Choice Angus beef displayed in a manner that transports one back to a time when we were on a first name basis with the grocer, the baker, and the butcher in our neighborhoods. Home baked pies are showcased in a grand antique pie case. Fresh produce drapes one side of an old wagon while candy entices youngsters from the other. Gourmet food items, cookbooks, signature jams and jellies, and homemade sausage beckon to shoppers from old cupboards.

Houser's renovation extended next door to what was the old post office before it closed in the 1970s. He transformed it into Jesse's Restaurant, which has now become one of the major culinary attractions along the Gulf Coast. House specialties include fresh seafood, meat dishes (including their award-winning Whiskey Steak), and a smattering of Louisiana-inspired Cajun and Creole dishes such as their etouffee and spicy gumbo. The restaurant also does a lively catering business, and is available for private parties.

"The old market held some cherished memories for us," Houser relates, "and we wanted to bring it back to its former position as a focal point of the community. Opening the restaurant next door completed the package. It's named after Jesse King, who worked at Moore Brothers for over 60 years and never missed a day's work."

That's what life was like for people in Magnolia Springs years ago, and thanks to the Houser family we can still get a glimpse of that era today. — Niki Sepsas

Magnolia River mail carrier Huey Collins, photo by Charlie Siefried (courtesy First National Bank of Baldwin County)

Magnolia Springs

The road that takes you from Highway 98 into Magnolia Springs is a step back in time. The small, romantic village of Magnolia Springs, principally settled by Creoles, awaits you.

Travel down Oak Street, roofed with Oak trees, which parallels the Magnolia River. Here you will find many homes, some very old, and some quite new. You will pass Magnolia Springs Bed and Breakfast, the Magnolia Springs Community Center, and St. Paul's Episcopal Chapel built in 1902 from pines harvested on the site. Across the street from the Chapel is The Moore Bros. Village Market. If you are hungry you won't be disappointed with the food at Jesse's, which adjoins the Market.

Residents along the Magnolia River are served by aquatic post, a mail by boat service, the only one of its kind in the United States. The 25-mile-long route, which dates from 1916, runs on both sides of the Magnolia all the way to Weeks Bay and Fish River. River Route Carriers, including one woman, make the trip in all kinds of weather.

The Magnolia River is tidewater, rising and falling with the daily tides and host to both fresh and saltwater fish. Down the river from the Magnolia River Bridge, you will find what is called "Devil's Hole," reported to be 75 feet deep and a favorite fishing spot for reds and specks.

Recipes

Magnolia Springs is located at the headwaters of the Magnolia River. In 1800 the Spanish granted the land that includes Magnolia Springs to turpentine still owner Joseph Collins. Through good times and bad, Magnolia Springs remained a place of hospitality as evidenced by the Magnolia Springs Bed and Breakfast, which was opened in a historic old house by David Worthington in December 1996.

David's Apple Dumplings

1 can   crescent rolls
1   Granny Smith Apple, peeled, cored and cut into 8
         quarters (can also use a pear)
         cinnamon, sprinkle to taste

Sauce: Warm the following three ingredients till dissolved
1 cup   orange juice
3/4 cup sugar
1/2 stick butter

Wrap 1/8 of apple with one piece of crescent roll and seal all edges. Place seam side down in Pyrex pan (9 x 13) Pour sauce over them and sprinkle with cinnamon. Cook at 350 degrees for 20-25 minutes until done. Baste dumplings with sauce in the pan before moving to plate. Drizzle a small amount of sweetened vanilla yogurt on top as icing. Makes 8 dumplings.

David's Eggs

8   eggs
1 can   green chilies
1 16 oz. tub of cottage cheese (lg. Curd, 4% milk fat)
8 oz.   sharp cheddar cheese

Shred cheese and coat with 2 tbsp. of flour. Beat eggs with green chilies, then add cottage cheese, then cheddar cheese and mix. Pour into 9 inch pie pan and bake at 350 degrees for 55-60 minutes.

Breakfast Pizza

1/2 lb. sausage
6   eggs beaten
1/4 cup milk
1 8 oz. crescent rolls
2 cups   hash browns
1 1/2 cps. four-cheese Mexican blend
3 tbsp. grated Parmesan cheese
         salt and pepper

Cook sausage and drain. Separate dough and spread out in a greased pizza pan; seal edges. Spoon sausage over dough, sprinkle with hash browns. Salt and pepper to taste. Combine eggs and milk and pour over sausage and hash browns. Sprinkle with four-cheese blend then finish with Parmesan cheese. Bake at 375 degrees for 25 minutes.

Shrimp Boat, *painting by Willoweise (courtesy of the artist)*

Recipes

Bay Shrimp Boil

Fill large pot 2/3 full with water. Add quartered onion, 8 celery stalks, 4 tbsp. salt, 6 halved lemons, and 1 bag Zatarain's Crab Boil. Bring to boil. Add washed, new potatoes and bring to boil. Add corn on the cob and return to boil. Add 5 pounds of shrimp and boil 6 minutes. Crabs can be added with shrimp, if desired. Remove from heat and enjoy.

Bon Secour

Nestled beneath old moss-draped oaks, the community of Bon Secour, the "safe harbor" founded by the French, still today cherishes its centuries of traditions of living from the sea.

Bon Secour was influenced by the French, Spanish, English and the Baltic Germans, but Jacque Cook, a Frenchman from Montreal, is given credit as the founder of Bon Secour around the 1800s. Cook named the area Bon Secour for the church which stands on a hill near the Canadian city and is called Notre Dame de Bon Secours. Seven generations of the Cook family have lived in the area.

When the Union blockades cut off supplies of salt coming from New England, Baldwin Countians, mostly women and children and old men, extracted salt from sea water. Fifteen salt houses located on the north shore of the lower Bon Secour River produced an average of 75 bushels of salt per day for the Confederate cause. Salt-starved people from all over Baldwin County came to Bon Secour for salt. Among blockade runners that transported salt to Mobile were the Ocean, Margaret Jane, St. Charles, Clara La Costa, and the War Eagle. When delivered, the commodity sold for $40 for a 60-pound bag and as high as $150 a bushel.

The Baltic Germans built the first Anglican Church, St. Peters, at the mouth of the Bon Secour River. The first Roman Catholic Church, Our Lady of Good Health, was dedicated about 1890. It was damaged by the storm of 1917, dismantled and moved to its present location. The church was given the name Our Lady of Bon Secour. Thomas Nelson founded a Baptist congregation as early as 1850.

For years, Bon Secour has been known for its oysters.

The earliest French maps of the area detailed the locations of rich oyster beds, a matter of great interest to the French world. Bon Secour Fisheries, owned and operated by the Nelson family, have been in Bon Secour for over a hundred years. Another well-known place to purchase fresh seafood is Billy's, located on the Bon Secour River.

Swift School is one of the oldest schools in Baldwin County. The school's beginning was at Miller's Bend, an 1850s settlement that was just west of the Bon Secour settlement. This school, known as Witt's School, was built next to the St. Peter's Episcopal Church by the Sea. In 1906 the Swift family moved to the area, built a sawmill and soon thereafter built a one-room schoolhouse across from the present day school where the Morgan's Chapel now stands. In 1916 five acres of land were given by the Swift family to build the present-day school with additions in 1922 and 1925.

Momma's Flowers, *painting by Linda Ledet (courtesy of Fidelis Studios)*

Middle Bay Lighthouse photo by Charlie Siefried (courtesy First National Bank of Baldwin County)

Live Oaks &
Gentle Folks

Page and Pallette

The Page & Palette in Orange Beach was opened in 1990 as a branch of the Fairhope store and remained a branch until the proprietor, Betty Joe Wolff, sold the Fairhope store to her ganddaughter. Although separate stores now, both strive to serve artists and book lovers with wonderful variety and service.

The beach store claims to be "the best book and artist supply store on the gulf coast!" Come see.

Gulf Shores

Where Baldwin County meets the sheltering seas of the Gulf of Mexico, the town of Gulf Shores has greeted generations of families seeking fun in the sun and surf of a quintessential shore town.

Here the world-famous sugar-white beaches, terrific hotels and condos and wonderful food combine with championship golf, superb fishing, and fun attractions, to create thousands of great experiences and stories.

A trip along Highway 98 will bring you through Gulf Shores, Orange Beach, Romar Beach, Ono Island and Perdido, Baldwin County's ultimate playground.

Tourism is Baldwin County's number one industry. In 2001, Baldwin County had 3.8 million visitors to the area with travel-related expenditures of $1.5 billion. State lodging taxes collected in the county amounted to $7 million. Employment in the county included 34,669 travel-related jobs with $632.3 million paid in wages and salaries. The community impact in Gulf Shores, Orange Beach and Foley shows 73 percent of all municipal revenue is directly attributable to visitor spending.

{The Annual National Shrimp Festival, produced by the Alabama Gulf Coast Chamber of Commerce, has been held during the second full weekend of October for 32 years.}

The Seagull, *watercolor by Blanche Sumrall* (courtesy of the artist)

Live Oaks &
Gentle Folks

Photo by Charlie Siefried (courtesy First National Bank of Baldwin County)

Pelicans,
watercolor by
Blanche Sumrall
(courtesy of the
artist)

Why They Call It Orange Beach

During the early 1900s, the most prominent thing on Orange Beach wasn't beachside condos, it was orange trees. Orange groves dotted the area, growing Satsuma oranges—small, hardy oranges that could survive winter cold. Eventually, the cold won out and the industry died away. But the name stuck.

The Dunes, *watercolor by Blanche Sumrall* (courtesy of the artist)

Recipes

Crab Soup

1/2 cup chopped green bell pepper
3/4 cup chopped celery
1/2 cup chopped onion
1/4 cup chopped parsley

Saute in 1/2 cup butter the peppers, celery and onions Add 1/4 cup flour. Cook approximately 1 to 2 minutes.
Add remaining ingredients:
2 cups milk
3 cups half and half
2 tsp. salt
1/4 tsp. white pepper
1/4 tsp. Tony Chachere's Creole seasoning
1/4 cup finely chopped parsley
4 cups green onions chopped
3 cups crab meat
2 cups fresh mushrooms sliced

Cook over low heat. Add sherry before serving if desired. 8 to 10 cup serving. Submitted by Elizabeth Rockwell

Romar Beach, *watercolor by Lucille Kubicek* (courtesy of Annette and Jim Lay)

Live Oaks & Gentle Folks

Crab a la Newburg

2 cups   crab meat
1/2 cup   butter
2 cups   cream
2 tbsp.   flour
4   eggs
3/4 tsp.   salt
          pepper to taste
          dash of cloves
1/2 tsp.   paprika
1/2 cup   dry sherry
          juice 1 lemon
1 tbsp.   brandy

Melt butter in iron skillet, but do not brown. Stir in crab meat gently and saute for one minute. Add lemon juice, stir in flour. Then add cream slowly, stirring constantly and lightly. When sauce is smooth, add salt, pepper, cloves, and paprika, and let mixture bubble five minutes.
Have ready the piping hot serving dish, hot plates, and toast points. Stir in the sherry. Beat the eggs just short of foaminess and stir in quickly. Add the brandy.
Serve with any dry white wine and any green salad with French dressing. Serves 4 to 6.
Submitted by Webb Denton

Hot Crabmeat Puffs

2 egg   whites
1 cup   mayonnaise
1 cup   fresh flaked white crab meat

Whip 2 egg whites until very stiff. Fold 1 cup mayonnaise into 1 cup fresh flaked white crab meat. Season and pile on small squares of toast or crackers.
Sprinkle with paprika and broil until puffy and lightly browned. Top with sprig of parsley, and pass to your guests while hot. Submitted by Julia V. Bullock

Shrimp Creole

2 lbs.   shrimp
1 lg.   onion (diced)
1   bell pepper
2 cups   celery
1 tsp.   celery seed
1   #3 can tomatoes
2 tbsp. chili sauce
         dash Worcestershire
2 tbsp. parsley (diced)
1 tsp.   salt
1 tsp.   garlic powder
1 tbsp. flour (browned)

Boil shrimp with salt and crab boil for 20 minutes, drain and clear. Cook bacon crisp, drain. Cook onion, pepper and celery until tender and slightly brown. Add tomatoes, chili sauce, salt, celery seed, garlic powder. Mix flour slowly, blend in kitchen bouquet to brown. Let simmer until all is tender and well blended together, stirring occasionally, Now add cooked shrimp and blend together about 5 minutes.
Serve over steaming rice.
Submitted by Dorothea Owen Miller

Quiet Beach, *watercolor by Willowweise* (courtesy of the artist)

Fort Morgan

The French, the English, the Spanish, and the Americans. Each nation has held what is now Fort Morgan. The first fortifications were built here on the tip of this 32-mile-long island back in 1559.

In the War of 1812 it was twice attacked. After a ferocious three-day battle, the British captured it, only to return the fortifications a few weeks later when it was discovered the Peace Treaty of Ghent had officially ended the war before the battle had been decided.

During the Civil War Fort Morgan figured prominently in the Battle of Mobile Bay, in which torpedoes and smoke screens were used for the first time, giving rise to Adm. Farragut's famous command, "Damn the torpedoes! Full speed ahead!" After the Confederate fleet surrendered, the fort held out for 19 days before it fell, on August 23, 1864. A Civil War Encampment re-enacts the Siege of Fort Morgan during the last weekend in August

The fort, a brick structure in fine condition, was built in 1818, based on a design by Michelangelo. The adjoining museum is a 1967 reconstruction of the 10-sided citadel, which was destroyed in 1864.

Fort Morgan photo by Charlie Siefried (courtesy First National Bank of Baldwin County)

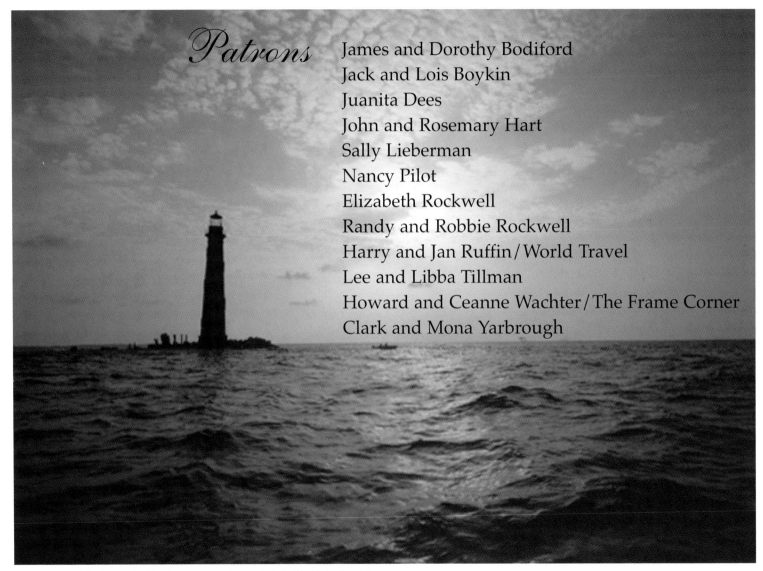

Patrons

James and Dorothy Bodiford

Jack and Lois Boykin

Juanita Dees

John and Rosemary Hart

Sally Lieberman

Nancy Pilot

Elizabeth Rockwell

Randy and Robbie Rockwell

Harry and Jan Ruffin/World Travel

Lee and Libba Tillman

Howard and Ceanne Wachter/The Frame Corner

Clark and Mona Yarbrough

Lighthouse photo by Charlie Siefried (courtesy First National Bank of Baldwin County)

Live Oaks Gentle Folks